Lay Theology

JOHN B. COBB Jr.

Chalice Press
St. Louis, Missouri

Biblical quotations, unless otherwise noted, are from the *New Revised Standard Version Bible*, copyright 1989, Division of Christian Education of the National Council of the Churches of Christ in the USA. Used by permission.

Cover design and illustration: Bob Watkins
Art Director: Michael Dominguez

10 9 8 7 6 5 4 3 2 1

Library of Congress Cataloging–in–Publication Data

Cobb, John B.
    Lay theology / John B. Cobb.
        p. cm.
    Includes bibliographical references.
    ISBN 0-8272-2122-3
    1. Theology, Doctrinal—Popular works. I. Title.
BT77.C564   1994   94-27738
230—dc20

Printed in the United States of America

Lay Theology

Preface

This book grows out of lectures delivered at Baldwin-Wallace College in February 1991 and at the First Presbyterian Church in Auburn, Alabama, in May 1993. There were three Baldwin-Wallace lectures, and the title of the series was "Whither Theology Now?" Auburn wanted four lectures, and I proposed the same title. It was while working on this second set of lectures that I realized that my real interest was not in speculating about where theology is in fact headed but in calling on laypeople to take their rightful place in the enterprise and identifying what that place is. It now seems to me that that place is more important than that of the professionals. The lectures began to gain more coherence as my real purpose and focus became clearer to me. I want to take this occasion to thank my hosts at both institutions for their invitations to speak and for their graciousness to me. The stimulus of each event encouraged and guided continuing revisions.

I have recently written another book also directed to laypeople. It is a workbook for doing theology. A reader of the present book who wants more specific guidance in becoming a good theologian may find help in *On Becoming a Thinking Christian* (Nashville: Abingdon Press, 1993). The two books are complementary. This one talks about the task. The other engages the lay theologian directly in it.

The fact that I have recently been writing and lecturing on this topic increasingly suggests that its importance has grown on me. That importance is discussed in the first chapter. Here I will say only that I see little hope for any of our oldline denominations if laypeople do not take up the theological task.

"Theology" is carefully defined in the body of the book. But "lay" is not. The distinction in my mind is not that between those who have been ordained and those who have not. It is between those who are church professionals and those who make their living or spend their lives in other ways.

Actually, the use of "professionals" in the text is usually narrower still. I am speaking primarily of those who earn their living studying and teaching theology. Most clergy do not devote much time to these activities and so function more as laypeople than as professionals with respect to theology. But there are also pastors and church officials who are not employed to teach but who nevertheless participate in the professional discussion. Exactly where the line is drawn is not important to the argument of the book. The book is written primarily for Christians engaged in work outside the church who are serious about their faith.

On the other hand, there is not likely to be a renewal of lay theology without the committed encouragement of pastors and other professional church leaders. I believe that there are many laypeople who, with such encouragement, could become enthusiastic about contributing to the theology of the church. But their experience of the church has not prepared them for this role. The renewal of lay theology is a task for the whole church. If this book can make any contribution to that task, I will rejoice.

Contents

The Renewal of Christian Thinking in the Church

The Importance of Theology's Renewal for the Church

"I'm not a theologian, I'm only a layperson."

"I'm not a theologian, I'm only a pastor."

How often we hear these disclaimers! And how sad it is that any Christian would find it necessary to make them! They tell us all too much about what has happened to theology—and to the church—in the past generation. Many Christians now think of theology as something done by authorities who then tell them what they are supposed to think. Other Christians think of theology as something esoteric and irrelevant to their actual lives. Most assume that theology is the work of professional theologians to whom the whole task has been relegated. A great many have little interest in how these specialists carry out their work.

1

It may be, of course, that those who hear "theology" in these ways are correct. Perhaps theology has a future only in official church teaching on one side, and in scholarly traditions transmitted and advanced in the academic world on the other. But this book is written in the hope that this is not the case. It proposes a future for theology in the church that does not depend on pronouncements handed down from on high, and it has little to say about theology's future in the academy. Instead, it calls for renewal of theology in the congregations, and it explains what sorts of theology can and should be carried on there. If that kind of renewal takes place, this will have a profound effect on official church pronouncements and on what happens among the scholars in the field. But that is not the topic of this book. The topic is laypeople doing theology again.

I choose this topic for two reasons. The first is the importance of such renewal for the church. This is the topic of this section. The second is the importance of such renewal for the world—the topic of the following section.

The time may be ripe for a reversal of a long-term decline of lay theology. In reaction to the abstract and remote character of much that has been done under the heading of "theology," most laypeople have decided that they can get along very well without it. Also, church leaders have decided that theology is divisive and that it is best to talk about other things. But gradually the realization is dawning that without widely shared convictions about the nature of reality, God, human beings, and the world, about what has happened in history, about what can be hoped for, and about what all this means for the way life is lived and public policy is developed, there is not much that the church can be or do. More and more people find the rhetoric of its scriptures, its hymns, and its liturgies alienating rather than uniting. Habits of loyalty to the institution are not enough.

The survival of a healthy Christianity depends on a vigorous dealing with theological issues on the part of Christians generally. That is a strong statement, and one that should rightly give us pause. If it is true, then much needs to be done, and done urgently, that is currently a very low priority in most denominations and most local churches.

Consider what happens when theology is not pursued by most of the people of the church, that is, what is happening now in our oldline Protestant denominations. When denominations face difficult decisions, they debate the alternatives in terms that are not distinctively Christian. Sometimes they appoint committees or commissions with the mandate to consider the issues theologically. And sometimes good work is done. But when representatives of the congregations vote on these issues in judicatories, their votes are determined far more by prejudices and preferences that reflect the general culture and their location in this culture than by serious wrestling with theological arguments proffered in the committee reports.

The committee reports are not always correct. Their theological content is often questionable and may itself be little more than a rationale to justify views that have, in fact, a nontheological origin. But their acceptance or rejection by the judicatory is usually little affected by the merits of the theological argument. Since nothing more than this is expected of denominational leadership, when the membership as a whole learn of the results of these votes, they do not take them as having any special authority. On the contrary, they see the official denominational decision as expressing just the opinions of those who happened to be present and voting. Such decisions have little effect on the attitudes of most church members.

As a result, denominations fragment into factions. This could result also from taking theology seriously. But then the fragments would have reason to believe that faithfulness to Christ has called them into existence. The current fragmentation expresses cultural and political differences rather than theological ones. It becomes harder and harder to discern what church life has to do with the gospel. Institutional survival more and more becomes the only shared goal of the oldline denomimations.

Even when denominations turn directly to the task of stating what they believe, the results are likely to be inauthentic. The task becomes the political one of finding a rhetoric to which all can subscribe. For the most part that consists in familiar language coming out of the denominations' traditions that does not have controversial implications for the present. Formulating doctrine thus is more a way of avoiding serious theology than advancing it.

The situation in local congregations is similar. When they face the need to make decisions, they have no history of theological reflection on which to draw. Hence the members draw on their personal and professional experience. Their discussion involves little serious engagement with the resources or demands of Christian faith. Or if someone does speak for a particular action in the name of faith, others may be intimidated into agreeing even against their better judgment. Few are prepared to challenge such an argument theologically.

Among the increasing number who recognize the unhealthiness and long-term danger of this situation, many call for a retrieval of older forms of belief. Less common is the realization that stemming this decline of lay theology cannot be primarily a matter of placing more emphasis on ancient creeds and confessions or the statements of denominational founders. It is true that any theological renewal will involve learning our history and wrestling seriously with ancient, authoritative pronouncements. But authentic renewal of lay theology does not occur by asking church people to accept ideas formulated long ago. It requires thinking now.

Too often we have forgotten that in the New Testament the commandment to love God is not limited to heart, soul, and strength. The New Testament adds "mind" (Matthew 22:37, Mark 12:30, and Luke 10:27). Probably in the Hebrew, "soul" included what we call mind, so the added term was not needed, but we can be glad that the writers of the Gospels make that explicit in their Greek translation. A depth-of-soul and warmth-of-heart religion cannot make up for the loss incurred when we do not think about who God is, what God does for us, and how we can best respond. Thinking about such matters is very different from accepting past ideas on authority. It involves critical appraisal of what is received from the past, and creative reflection in the present.

Unfortunately, many Christians have ignored this commandment to love God with all our minds. Some have been troubled by its divisiveness. Others are intellectually lazy. Still others have been intimidated by institutional control of orthodoxy or the claims of professional specialists. The result has been a widespread preference for a mindless love of God.

The twentieth century has witnessed many movements embodying intense feelings and sacrifical devotion that have been massively destructive. Some of these have made an appeal to Christ to justify their destructive approach to outsiders and sometimes to their own members. Fervor and depth of feeling are admirable in themselves. But if they are not directed by critical reflection, they usually do more harm than good. And when, in recognition of this danger, feeling and fervor are reduced, very little remains. Much of the church's present life can be plotted on a line extending between fanaticism and lukewarmness.

The Importance of Theology's Renewal for the World

The first reason for urging a renewal of lay theology is its importance for the church. Without it the church loses its soul. The second reason for urging such renewal is its importance for the world. One may say that the healthy survival of humanity depends on Christians dealing with theological issues while Jews and Muslims, Hindus and Buddhists deal freshly and seriously with analogous issues deriving from their traditions. These strong statements are not without support in what is going on around the world today.

At present, strife in India, in Sri Lanka, in Ireland, and in the Middle East is conducted under the banner of religion. Religious differences play a central role in the struggle between Orthodox Serbs, Roman Catholic Croats, and Muslims in Bosnia. On the whole, religious communities seem to be more part of the world's problems than part of their solution.

Much of the role that religions play in these conflicts is inseparable from the cultures with which they are associated. For example, the Protestant-Catholic strife in Ireland is not directly about the differences between Protestant and Catholic teaching. Similarly, conflicts between Hindus and Muslims in India and between Hindus and Buddhists in Sri Lanka are not primarily over specifically religious beliefs. Nevertheless, the religious dimension is important in all these struggles.

Some of the most intractable of global political problems center around Israel. There the Jewish need for a Jewish state has resulted in terrible suffering and oppression for the Palestinian people. These are problems to which religious beliefs have contributed a great deal. Among the contributing factors are: the long history of Christian persecution of Jews, a persecution explicitly grounded in Christian doctrine; the Jewish belief in rightful ownership of the land of Israel, a belief explicitly grounded in Jewish scriptures; tardy recognition of guilt toward the Jews on the part of many Christians; and belief on the part of some Christians that the return of Jews to Israel is a part of the coming apocalypse. Also important is the fact that some of those Christian teachings that have given rise to persecution in the past are still in effect, so that Jews have reason to fear that Christendom may renew its hostility. In addition, Christian and Jewish prejudices against Islam continue to distort interpretations of the situation.

The most serious danger that religious belief poses to the planet is its tendency to set one community against others. That means, as a minimum, that better understanding of other religious communities is important for all. To limit ourselves to the communities that are involved in the conflicts in the Middle East, Americans need to understand Judaism and Islam as well as Christianity, and that means also that we need to understand several major forms of all these traditions. If we do not, national policies, even when successful at one level, will continue to exacerbate the deeper problems.

In much of the nineteenth and twentieth centuries, cultured opinion tended to dismiss the religious communities as of diminishing importance in world affairs. Recently the tide has turned. The importance of religious conflicts, as emphasized above, is one reason, but not the only one. More and more people, regardless of their personal faith or lack of faith, are recognizing that, for good or ill, religious feelings and commitments are here to stay. Secularism is not, as so many had thought, the inevitable result of increasing knowledge and education. It is, instead, a precarious, and even abnormal, condition that involves cutting off certain ordinary dimensions of thought and feeling.

Decades of ridicule and persecution of religious believers by Communist governments have served only to intensify religious interest in Eastern Europe and to give traditional religious leaders greater status. Christianity has flourished in China despite, or because of, government opposition. The importance of changing religious beliefs in Latin America has been recognized by even the most unsympathetic secular observers. The resurgence of Islam is a world-historical event that influences the foreign policies of all nations. The power of the religious right in the United States is regularly discussed in the news.

The beliefs that are most important, whether of Protestants, of Catholics, of Jews, of Muslims, of Hindus, or of Buddhists, are those that actually shape the lives and feelings of large numbers of people. They are not ideas discussed only by professionals in ivory towers. The theology that is crucial for the future of the planet is the theology by which masses of people live.

Fortunately, this is not static. The dominant beliefs and attitudes of Christians, Jews, and Muslims today are not the same as they were a hundred or a thousand years ago. Some of the change is caused simply by changed circumstance. But some of it is also brought about by reflection. The reflection of believers about their beliefs plays a crucial role in history. Among Christians this kind of reflection is called theology. Some of this reflection has been that of professional leaders. But unless it enters into the mainstream of thinking among believers, it will not bring about the changes on which the healthy survival of humanity depends.

There can be no question of the importance of broader and more objective understanding of the several religious traditions if religious communities are to live at peace with one another. Fortunately, there are now many scholars who are giving their lives to this kind of understanding. Many universities have religious studies departments that specialize in offering objective information and sympathetic understanding of the various religious communities in the world. Those Christians who are willing to be informed have a large quantity of literature at their disposal.

In departments of philosophy one often finds instruction in philosophy of religion. This is also an objective study of religion, but with a difference. The focus is on the value and validity of religious beliefs. Sometimes there are proposals from philosophers as to how the apparent diversity of beliefs—so divisive in the real world—can be overcome or dealt with in a way that would overcome mutual rejections.

This work in the history and philosophy of religion is a secular contribution for which Christians and members of other religious communities should be grateful. But by itself this secular scholarship will not change the situation much. Human beings do not exist outside or above the religious traditions, viewing them from without. We are immersed in communities that shape our values and our lives by their traditions. What is learned by secular scholarship must be incorporated into these traditions if it is to redirect religious energies away from mutual hostility. This incorporation of new knowledge and understanding into ongoing communities of faith is a theological task.

Thus far I have spoken of the danger that religious communities pose to peace. There is no doubt that religion does play this role. It provides a rallying cry for communities of believers against other communities. It sanctions and even sacralizes the cause for whose sake it is invoked. This makes compromise and reconciliation more difficult.

Fortunately, this is not the only role of religious traditions. Within each religious community there are also teachings that call for understanding, respect for all human beings, and peace. There are principles of self-criticism and warnings against fanaticism. These positive teachings are usually far more central to the religious traditions than the ones that become the battle cries of one community against another. Furthermore, these teachings are playing an important role today alongside the others.

In Sri Lanka, the Buddhist leader of the Sarvodaya movement there, Sri Ariyaratne, works diligently and sacrificially for reconciliation with the alienated Hindus. In Israel there are prophetic Jewish critics of the government whose voices are repeatedly raised against injustices to the Palestinians despite their own desire for a secure Jewish homeland. In Christendom there are thinkers who work committedly to free Christianity from its deeply entrenched anti-Jewish teachings. Bringing these central principles of the religious traditions to bear on what is going on today is also theological work.

In a secular world that has difficulty identifying any values around which to organize action, the religious traditions offer an extremely important corrective. They can without apology condemn injustice, point out false assumptions operative in society, and guard against denial of human dignity. Their rich traditions offer essential guidance to a confused society.

The most global problem facing humanity at present is that of environmental degradation accompanied by increasing human population and wasteful practices on the part of the rich. Many of those who have been most keenly aware of the need for change originally took their stand outside and over against the religious traditions. Increasingly they have recognized that no adequate human response is possible without the support of religious communities. They have also come to see that these communities have resources for making the needed responses.

Meanwhile, members of these communities have been working within them toward the same ends. They see that their own traditions do call them to oppose the wasteful exploitation of the earth and, instead, to respect and appreciate it. Increasingly their agreement on this fundamental point has gained public and visible expression. This, too, has required theological work within each community and especially within Christianity. To move beyond recognition of a general truth to the needed reorientation of life and thought in the several traditions will require much more extensive theological reflection. This cannot be the work of only a few specialists.

Church Theology and Academic Theology

At the beginning of this chapter I argued that a renewal of theology is essential if the church is to respond in a Christian way to the challenges it faces. In the subsequent section I argued that such renewal is indispensable for the healthy survival of humanity. The theology in question is not, must not be, primarily an academic discipline pursued by a handful of professionals. It can only perform its indispensable function if it becomes part of the ordinary life of the church.

Theology, as I use this term, differs from religious studies and from philosophy of religion in two main ways. First, whereas the latter are defined by their subject matter, namely, religion, the former is defined by its perspective, the Christian faith. Christian theology works from an intentionally Christian point of view. Many of those who engage in religious studies and philosophy of religion are Christian, but they attempt to prevent their personal faith from affecting their scholarly work. Theologians, in contrast, try to think as *Christians*, and to recognize that what they see and affirm is shaped by this perspective. Of course, they can and should be informed by what religious studies and philosophy of religion contribute. But *theology* is intentional Christian thinking.

A further word of explanation is needed here. We sometimes speak of Jewish, Muslim, or even Buddhist theology. I personally have no problem with this language. It means for me intentional Jewish, Muslim, or Buddhist thinking. But most Jews, Muslims, and Buddhists do find the term awkward. It identifies for them a mode of reflection that is not characteristic of their heritage, one that, if practiced at all, is learned or copied from Christians. Hence, despite the apparently discriminatory character of this usage, when the word *theology* stands alone, it refers to Christian theology. If representatives of other traditions choose to use this term to describe what they do, they usually distinguish it as Jewish or Buddhist theology. If in the future more Jews, Muslims, and Buddhists come to accept the term *theology* as describing some of what they do, the term will become generic, and the Christian practice of this activity will always be named

"Christian theology." This change will be hastened if there is wide acceptance of the understanding of *theology* as thinking that is intentionally informed by participation in a particular religious community.

Second, just because theology is defined by its point of view rather than by its subject matter, its subject matter is much broader than that of religious studies or philosophy of religion. Theology does, of course, treat the phenomena of religion and the religious traditions and communities. Christian theology pays special attention to the particular tradition that provides its perspective. But theologians deal with any aspect of reality that concerns Christians, any aspect that seems important to them. Hence my full definition of *theology* is "intentional Christian thinking about important matters."

This definition of *theology* shows still more clearly why it should be the activity of the whole church rather than of a special group of professionals. If one is a Christian, one should think about important matters in a Christian way. The alternative would be to define one's Christianity only in terms of certain practices, such as prayer, Bible reading, and church attendance, with no expectation of their affecting the remainder of one's life.

Christians who do not engage in theology are not free of theological ideas. Their attitudes on many moral and public issues are informed by inherited beliefs of which they may be hardly conscious. Beliefs of this sort are what often lead to hostility toward other communities and lack of respect for the earth. The choice is not between thinking theologically or avoiding theology altogether. It is between theological reflection and unconscious dogmatism.

The exclusion of Christian reflection from life is not a real possibility for Christians. The problem is that, in the contemporary context of specialization and fragmentation, Christians find theology difficult and preoccupy themselves with other matters. They get their ideas about psychology from the psychologists, about sociology from the sociologists, about history from the historians, about science from the scientists, about economics from the economists. There are few important matters about which they expect to be helped by the professional theologians. Theology is viewed as one specialization among others, only less interesting, important, or relevant than most. Meanwhile, the practice of thinking about whether ideas are Christian fades away. This is a recipe for the decadence we are now experiencing in the North Atlantic oldline churches.

I am not describing this situation with the intention of blaming the churches or Christians in general. If anyone is to blame, it is the members of my own guild—the professional theologians. Too many of us have devoted ourselves to the issues posed by the intellectual history of the West rather than to the issues facing the planet, the church, and the individual Christian. In dealing with our scholarly problems, we have addressed ourselves to one another. In all of this we have not been worse than other academic guilds, but we have been little better. And as a result, "theology" has taken on the connotation of abstruseness and irrelevance. There are, of course, historical reasons for this development. To understand our present situation and to find ways to go beyond it, it is helpful to understand this history.

In the early church academic theology and church theology were not widely separated. Most lay Christians cared deeply about their beliefs and knew what they were. But with the rapid expansion of Christianity after the Constantinian establishment, more and more people were baptized without serious theological instruction. They brought into the popular piety of the church many beliefs and practices that derived from other sources. Most were illiterate and quite selective of the aspects of Christian teaching that they really appropriated. This meant that the clergy had the primary responsibility to maintain and advance the tradition. The laity were not required to understand much themselves as long as they accepted the authority of the clergy in matters of faith.

In the later Middle Ages, with the growth of cities and a literate middle class, lay Christians claimed a larger role in the church. They challenged the clerical monopoly of theological knowledge. The Reformation can be seen as part of this movement. The Reformers called for all Christians to read the Bible for themselves and to be responsible for their own faith. Protestants worked hard to extend literacy so that laypeople would not be dependent on the clergy for knowledge of the Bible. The gap between clergy and laity was significantly reduced.

Beginning in the Renaissance, many of the thinkers who were most influential in shaping the religious thought of their times were laypeople. Some of their work was outside the church and critical of Christianity as a whole, whereas others were seeking to purify and transform Christianity. There was considerable anticlericalism, especially in Catholic countries, as the clergy were perceived as seeking to maintain their prerogatives without justification.

There were also religious revivals among the common people, such as that of Wesley in Great Britain, in which most of the preachers were themselves lay. As denominations that grew out of these revivals began to raise educational standards among their clergy, new movements without these standards came into being. This pattern has continued to the present day, and it has been especially important in shaping religious life in the United States. Also, the education of clergy, even when required by denominations, often assumes less intellectual capacity and interest than comparable education for other professions. Instead of the clergy being the educated segment of the population, they are, on the whole, less able to provide intellectual leadership than many of the laity.

Extensive involvement of laypeople in theology continued into the twentieth century. Much of the debate about evolutionary theory was conducted by laypeople. They played a large role in interpreting the global mission movement and the social gospel. Arguments about the issues distinguishing the denominations were a normal part of lay activity. Church publishers continued to put out serious theological materials for laypeople past the middle of the twentieth century.

Unfortunately, during the second half of the twentieth century the education of the laity has moved away from relevance to their faith. The research university has replaced the liberal arts college, and religious issues are thoroughly compartmentalized in separate departments. Most laypeople study in secular institutions that encourage specialization in fields quite remote from theology. Church colleges tend to follow secular models. The only place where most laypeople are exposed to intentionally Christian thinking is in the church. But in most churches the professional staff is not equipped to encourage intentional Christian thinking at the level at which many members engage in thinking elsewhere. What is presented to laypeople as theology rarely grips or challenges them or encourages their serious involvement.

One reason that so few pastors understand their ministry as theological is that the theology taught in their seminaries does not respond to the questions of laypeople or the issues that arise in church life. Their professors have been preoccupied with classical debates or with questions raised in the course of modern intellectual history. These questions are far from irrelevant to the real beliefs by which many laypeople live, but the connection is rarely obvious, and few pastors are skilled in making them. As noted above, the very word *theology* has come to be used chiefly for the work of these professional seminary professors and identifies an activity remote from both pastors and laypeople.

There remains a range of issues with which the church must deal theologically. For example, ecumenical cooperation requires mutual understanding among denominations. Issues about ordination and the sacraments require reflection about the tradition. Changes in society force churches to reconsider traditional views, either reaffirming or changing them. Questions arise out of the lives of laypeople to which some answer must be given. In these ways theological concerns force themselves on the church. Accordingly, alongside the academic theology of the seminary classes, there is also a church theology.

There has been, thus, in recent times, a double tradition. There is the tradition of church theology that deals with current questions. It does so primarily on the basis of theological formulations that predate the rise of modern science and the historical consciousness. There is also the tradition of Christian intellectuals who wrestled with these new issues. Here the focus is especially on the great thinkers of central Europe in the nineteenth and early twentieth centuries and those who continue their discussion today. Of course, the two traditions have interacted, but for the most part they have remained separate and are so today.

For a brief period in the middle of the twentieth century, the modern academic tradition and the ongoing church tradition coalesced in the person of Karl Barth. He was widely viewed as the heir and transformer of the academic tradition, while at the same time addressing the issues posed in and by the church. His work profoundly influenced the way Protestant denominations and conciliar groups thought and acted. However we evaluate particular features of his teaching, the integration of church theology and academic theology was an achievment much to be admired.

Rudolf Bultmann performed a similar service in relation to a very important part of the academic tradition—biblical scholarship. That scholarship has often prided itself on its objectivity and historical rigor in ways that removed it from direct relevance in the shaping of Christian life. Bultmann was the acknowledged leader of New Testament scholars. At the same time, he interpreted the Bible in the interest of preaching. Again, however one may judge the details of his exegetical work, this accomplishment deserves utmost respect.

Subsequently, this integration has broken down, both in New Testament scholarship and in theology generally. This may be especially true in the United States. The living tradition of academic scholarship and theology is less and less interested in relating to the church. And the church is increasingly captive to anti-intellectual elements and to older authorities. The problem for those of the church's professional theologians who want to participate in both traditions is acute.

What happened? In the sixties there was an explosion of discontent with the Barthian synthesis of the academic and church traditions. Radical theology, Black theology, Latin American liberation theology, and feminist theology all arose with sharp and harsh criticisms of "the tradition." During the same period we became aware of Christian responsibility for the Holocaust and of how pervasively anti-Jewish teaching permeated our heritage. Dialogue with representatives of other religious traditions forced us to realize how parochial we have been. Looking at ourselves from the perspective of primal peoples, especially Native Americans, also evoked reappraisal of our received habits of mind. We came to see how repressive our teachings about sexuality had been, and we were compelled to deal with the issues posed by the sexual revolution. We recognized that Western Christian teaching had distracted attention from what human beings have done to the environment, and even encouraged its mindless exploitation.

As a result, many academic professionals gave up on the Barthian synthesis and returned to their specialized work, and much of the church leadership sought refuge in familiar patterns of thought and life. Revolutionary proposals claimed attention on both sides, but were contained and marginalized in both academia and the church. Changes have occurred in both, but not in such a way as to bring them together.

To blame professors and scholars for our present confused situation is hardly more useful than blaming denominational leaders or other Christians. But now that the devastating results of our specialization and fragmentation are clear, we are all to blame if we fail to reflect on how a healthier condition can be restored to the church. That will consist not in mutual recrimination, but in working together to redefine theology and to become good theologians, that is, to think well as Christians about what is important for individual believers, for our churches, and for the planet.

Because academic disciplines are defined by their subject matters, theology in the university is often limited to the study of its own history. This was not true in the early church, the Middle Ages, or the Reformation. Certainly the theological tradition is important, even central. But in those days Christians assumed that there should be Christian teaching about the social, political, and economic orders as well. Indeed, no important question was off-limits to Christian reflection.

Roman Catholicism has continued this tradition to some extent. Protestants, however, have tended to accept, even encourage, the division of responsibility. Luther's doctrine of the two kingdoms has allowed some Protestants to limit Christian concern to the spiritual kingdom and remain silent with respect to the important issues faced in the earthly kingdom, even if Luther himself did not do this. There was more resistance to this separation among Calvinists. But with the emergence of the secular state and tolerance of diverse religious communities within it, the tendency to restrict Christian reflection to specifically religious topics increased. The social gospel was a massive protest against this narrowness, but it has faded. In the academic world, departmentalization is the order of the day, and, as an academic discipline, theology has accepted segregation.

The definition of theology here proposed is a protest against this narrow delimitation of theology. The protest is encouraged by the several liberation theologies, none of which have accepted restriction to disciplinary boundaries.

Indeed, the renewal of lay theology for which I am calling is modeled by the liberation theologies.

One proposal for the renewal of lay theology in the church could well be that we should extend the approach of liberation theology further and further through the church. However, this is not what is envisaged in the following chapters. Before considering the proposals made in them, it will be useful, even imperative, to consider what has been gained from liberation theologies, and to recognize the rich potential they continue to offer the church. I have no doubt that many Christians, indeed, an increasing number, are called to serve the church by pursuing and elaborating these liberation theologies and by developing new ones. I am writing this book not to discourage or oppose this continuing activity, but to suggest some parallel or correlative modes of Christian reflection that are open to those whose place in society makes direct contribution to liberation theology inappropriate.

Liberation Theologies

What, then, is "liberation theology"? Perhaps a better question is: what is a liberation theology? One of the main points of liberation theologians is that all thinking is deeply shaped by its social location. If one writes as if one's point of view were generically human, objective, or neutral, as if one could speak for everyone, one is likely to be presenting the position of the dominant group as if it were normative for all. Men should acknowledge that what they see is shaped by their maleness. Whites should recognize that their experience and resultant perceptions differ from that of colored peoples. A white male cannot speak for people in general. The pretense to doing so has intensified the oppression of the others.

To acknowledge that one's thinking is formed by particular circumstances is not to weaken it. Indeed, the liberation theologians have shown how rich is the consequence for theology of recounting the specificities of the situation and describing both how Christianity has thus far operated in this situation and how it could or should operate. Much that had been simply invisible to most of us, including those in that situation, has been unveiled by this approach.

When the situation that is described is one of oppression, then the second main tenet of liberation theologians comes into play. The gospel calls for liberation of the oppressed. This fact has long been obscured by the traditional individualistic preoccupation with sin and forgiveness. Few liberation theologians deny that we are all sinners in need of forgiveness. Indeed, they expose much sin of which we had been too little aware! But they do point out that the exclusive focus on individual sinfulness has obscured other equally important biblical emphases. They show that these other emphases are more relevant to the most urgent problems in the lives of hundreds of millions of people. To emphasize sin and forgiveness alone encourages the oppressed to think that they deserve their suffering and should accept it as part of their punishment. Christianity then ceases to be good news. Nothing is more important than the recovery of its message that this oppression is against God's will, that God sides with the oppressed against the oppressor and works with them for liberation.

The nature and causes of oppression vary greatly. Blacks have experienced oppression chiefly because of white racism. Since this has left most of them poor, class analysis has also been relevant, but it has been secondary. They find rich resources for responding to oppression in their Christian and cultural history and in their existing churches. They show that the Bible that has so often been used against them was in fact written from the perspective of the oppressed. This opens up whole new ways of understanding the Scriptures and of identifying God's present working in the world.

Latin American liberation theologians have analyzed their situation primarily in terms of class. In Latin America a ruling elite has exploited peasants and workers alike. It has controlled the church, so that until recently the church was primarily an instrument for gaining the cooperation of the poor in their own oppression. In order to allow the liberating word of the gospel to work among the poor, it has been necessary to invent a new institution, the base community, where the poor can tell their stories, relate the Bible to their lives, and claim God's promises.

Christian feminists have shown not only that Christianity has been complicit in the overwhelming patriarchy of the inherited tradition, but also that it has built patriarchal thinking into its theology. Furthermore, this is not a process that began in post-biblical times, such as that of the "church fathers." It is also part of the inheritance from Judaism. There is no simple appeal to biblical authority against traditional distortions. Although some Christian feminists establish separate institutions, these do not work for them as the Black church works for Blacks or the base communities work for the oppressed in Latin America. Most Christian feminists, therefore, have to struggle in and through the lives of ordinary congregations, so to transform them that the liberating word for women can become effective. Many have abandoned this struggle as hopeless. The church as a whole is deeply indebted to those who stay and keep trying.

Once these models were established, it became easier for other Christians to formulate analogous theologies in other social locations. Perhaps the most richly developed is Minjung theology in Korea. Koreans have suffered a long history of oppression from their neighbors, China and Japan. The people have also suffered from a rigid class structure within Korean society. Women have suffered additionally from systematic subordination to men. Koreans have named their inner response to all this oppression as *han*. For them, release from this han, both by cultural and religious means, and also by changing the structures and behavior that produce it, is the liberation they seek through the gospel.

Black women have found that their double oppression as Blacks and as women requires that they distinguish their theology from both Black and feminist theology. They call it womanist theology. Asian and Latin American women are also finding their distinctive voice. African liberation theologies are different still.

A third point of commonality in liberation theologies is an emphasis on concreteness and particularity. Often this is attained by telling the stories of those who have suffered from oppression. These make clear both the nature of the oppression and how people have survived in spite of it. For many liberation theologians, it is as important to see God working in the events recounted in these stories as to find God in the history recorded in the Bible.

Involving the Whole Church

What is the meaning of liberation theology for those who do not now define their thought in this way? The first possibility is that they should join in one of these movements. Many who fear to be thought extreme or aggressive if they associate with one of the liberation movements, or who have thought that these movements are not orthodox, or unacceptable for some other reason, are called to overcome their fears and hesitations. They have much to gain, and they may be able to contribute more to the community as a whole if they give themselves more fully to the liberation of the group to which they belong.

A second possibility is that some may be inspired to help to create new liberation theologies within the church. An example may be gay men. Whereas lesbians have a clear and strong place within the feminist movement, including the Christian part of that movement, gay liberation is still primarily outside the church. Despite a few efforts to formulate a gay liberation theology, little has been achieved. Yet there are hundreds of thousands of gays within the churches, they are among the most oppressed people in our society, and Christian teaching continues to play a major role in sanctioning that oppression. If the gospel is truly good news to the oppressed, this good news needs to be made clear in this instance. Furthermore, we have learned from the other liberation movements that a liberation theology cannot be produced by those in power for the benefit of the oppressed. It must be the work of those who suffer the oppression.

Many other groups experience oppression of various sorts. In some cases it makes sense to develop liberation theologies giving voice to their stories and the implications of those stories for Christian thinking. Such groups include those who have handicapping conditions such as deafness, blindness, or loss of use of some of their limbs. They include also many of the elderly who are often cast aside as useless burdens in our society. Those who are poorly educated or illiterate constitute another such group. Today, after a period of power, industrial workers are again being dramatically exploited. But in each case those who feel oppressed because of their condition must make their own decision as to whether the situation calls for systematic effort to articulate the implications of their oppression theologically.

The process of extending the understanding of oppression can go much further. White middle-class males in the North Atlantic countries can truthfully point out that their power is very limited. They are channeled into particular courses of life whether they like them or not. Their jobs are often pressure-filled and insecure. The vast majority of them do not belong to the true "ruling elite." Even those few who do may be profoundly frustrated by the course of events. Everyone feels some hurt from lack of support or approval by society as a whole or by the church. There is a value in telling these stories and thinking of them in relation to biblical ones.

On the other hand, developing liberation theologies for the rich and powerful would be absurd. Indeed, it would probably be counterproductive for poorer and less powerful white males who feel that they are oppressed by affirmative action to organize as a Christian liberation movement. There may be something to gain from the predominantly white men's movement now in the news, but whether this should give rise to a male liberation theology remains problematic. It is true that this society, like all civilizations, is oppressive of all its members in some respects. But the oppression experienced by the powerless is so different from that experienced by those who exercise dominant power that these distinctions need to be kept in mind.

One reason for doubt that all Christians should develop Christian theology from their personal experience of being oppressed is that this is not the only important aspect of the experience of Christians. There is also the experience of oppressing others and being involved in other forms of sin for which forgiveness is needed. There are problems of doubt and incredulity when faith confronts the massive unjust suffering in life. There are challenges to faith from the modern scientific worldview. And there are the needs for pastoral and community support experienced by all in the crises to which all lives are subject.

In addition, there are public needs that must be addressed whether or not they are articulated by any oppressed group of Christians. Two examples will suffice. First, in this time after the Holocaust, Christian theology must be freed of its anti-Judaism. This work cannot be done by Jews. It must be done by Christians out of repentance for our oppression of Jews. There is no assurance that the several liberation theologies will deal adequately, or even appropriately, with this need.

Second, as the environmental crisis forces itself more and more on our attention, care for the earth cannot be subordinated to the liberation of the oppressed. Increasingly, liberation theologians are recognizing the importance of considering this dimension of theology. But it is also urgent that white male North Atlantic theologians take up the issue in ways that make sense to us.

Finally, we need to note the inherent limitation in the liberation approach. Emphasizing the diverse forms of oppression can lead to diffuseness and fragmentation in the church's program. The church is in need of centripetal forces as well as the centrifugal ones. Some Christians need to take responsibility for the healthy and creative ongoing life of the community as a whole. Some Christians must acknowledge the dominant tradition as their heritage and work from that point of view to help the church to repent of our collective crimes. Some Christians should address the global issues of the day as representatives of the whole Christian community.

This is not a program to be set in opposition to the liberation theologies. When the church defines what is healthy and creative without hearing what the liberation theologians are saying, it ends up with what is unhealthy and discreative. Nevertheless, the program of the church as a whole cannot be decided by any one liberation theology or indeed only by liberation theologies collectively. The chapters that follow are calling for a somewhat different kind of theology to be pursued throughout the church.

Liberation theologians can rightly point out that the social location of the author is that of a white, North American male belonging to one of the oldline Protestant denominations. This kind of point is sometimes made in order to discredit what is said. There is some justification for this. We white, North American males have said and written so much that is insensitive to the distortions introduced when we take our perspective as normative that our critics are right to warn against this danger. It should be kept in mind in reading what follows.

But we white, North American, Protestant males do share in responsibility for the future of the church. That responsibility is heightened by our traditional position of power and privilege. We cannot exercise that responsibility well without listening to what others say. But having listened, we, too, must share in making proposals about how the church, as the church, can and should respond. We are joined in this by those women and minorities who are committed to the healthy continuation of the church as a whole and not only to the liberation of the oppressed groups to which they belong.

The chapters that follow do not pretend to describe all the ways in which Christians can respond theologically. They unabashedly present a set of proposals in terms of my own convictions. I stand in the theological tradition that is called process theology or process-relational theology. At times, especially in Chapter 4, I will explain openly how that plays itself out in these proposals. But most of what is said is not dependent on this particular perspective. Persons in other theological traditions may agree with much of it. There are few ideas important to the church on which a single theological tradition owns a patent!

Chapter 2 calls for practical theology in the congregations, and it proposes ways in which it can be introduced or strengthened there. These proposals are quite mundane. I believe they are also quite realistic. For laypeople to begin a process of thinking as Christians about the affairs of their personal lives and their congregations is scary to church professionals, since the theologies they bring to bear may not always appear to me or to other professionals to be adequate or healthy. But this is a risk the church must take if it is to be renewed. My own conviction is that in the process of developing practical theology the beliefs will become not only more relevant but also more Christian.

Chapter 3 extends practical theology to less accustomed domains. As our society has become more and more specialized, we have given less and less attention as Christians to the ways we make our living, organize our institutions, and structure our society. The Christianization of our lives has become limited to personal, familial, and churchly matters.

But many of the decisions that determine what happens at these levels are in fact made in other institutions. We need to consider what it means to carry out our business and professional lives as Christians, and how institutions and society as a whole should be changed. This requires critical analysis of the assumptions that now shape institutions and social order. Laypeople are best equipped to give leadership in all of this.

The first three chapters emphasize the importance of lay theology in some separation from the work of professional theologians. But the goal must be to bring these closer together. The problems with which professional theologians have dealt are important for the church as a whole. We professionals need to display this relevance and to make our work much more accessible. Lay theologians need to see the importance of dealing with the issues that have preoccupied professionals. Chapter 4 suggests ways of understanding how to deal with the tradition in which laypeople can share and which can draw together the work of professional and lay Christians.

2

Theology as Practical Christian Thinking

Beginning Where We Live

If laypeople are to recover their role as theologians, they can best begin with the issues that most immediately concern them. For most of them, the best starting point is with the questions that arise in everyday life. From there they can proceed to considering other issues that confront the church locally, regionally, and globally.

All serious Christians engage in this kind of thinking at least episodically. We try to behave in a Christian manner toward others, and that requires some reflection as to what a Christian manner may be. We want to bring up our children in a Christian way, and that too requires reflection. We believe that sexuality is good, but that much of what goes on in contemporary sexual practice is dangerous and destructive, and we want to find a Christian way. A member of the fam-

29

ily is dying in a painful way, and we want to know whether we as Christians should insist on protracting the dying process as long as possible.

In some very conservative and sectarian churches, a detailed code of conduct is spelled out and labeled Christian, and members are under pressure to think about how their lives conform to these "Christian" requirements. Some spiritual disciplines raise consciousness about how the details of daily life fit the Christian pattern or spirit. Some Christians who are keenly conscious of the social issues of the day look at all they do in these terms.

A great deal of preaching embodies or encourages practical Christian thinking. Models of Christian life and action are offered; solutions to life's problems are suggested; particular attitudes are commended. Occasionally there is tough-minded wrestling with difficult issues.

This means that when theology is understood as practical Christian thinking, most Christians can recognize it as part of their lives. It is hard to deny that we are all theologians! The problem is that we are not all good theologians. When we do think about the relevance of our faith, we sometimes think simplistically and superficially, and there are many aspects of our lives in which we make decisions without considering their relation to our faith.

The call to be good theologians could easily be misunderstood as calling for a style of life that is in fact undesirable. It may sound as though one should problematize every situation and delay response until one can think it through as a Christian. This would be highly artificial and destructive. Spontaneity would be gone. It is far better that we try to become persons of Christian integrity and sensitivity and act accordingly. The emphasis is rightly placed on Christian character rather than on constant reflective decision making. Most Christian action does not involve practical Christian thinking at the time of the action. Most of it is habitual.

But this does not minimize the importance of practical Christian thinking. First, this thinking plays a role in the formation of Christian habits. Second, it is important to reconsider habits from time to time. Some habits of Christians are not Christian habits. Also, habits that seemed Christian before our consciousness was raised by Black power or women's liberation or the deterioration of the environment do not appear Christian now. Fresh reflection is needed in the formation of different habits. Third, life repeatedly confronts us with new situations that demand something other than either habitual or purely spontaneous responses.

There is very little instruction in most of our churches on how to engage in practical Christian thinking. This is partly because there are no easily taught rules. There was a time when some preachers might encourage Christians to think what Jesus would do in their situation, or to follow the golden rule, or to pray for guidance, or to search the Scriptures. That is all good advice, but it tends to cut short reflection on the complexities of the problems. Today we might emphasize being sure that we consider these complexities both within the specific situation and between it and others. Sometimes a full analysis suffices to guide the response. But not always. More is needed.

That "more" is not the same in each instance. Different issues call for reflection of different types in different directions. There can be no exhaustive catalog of possible issues. Practical Christian thinking is learned in practice. Still, it is possible to give examples of situations in which it is needed and to encourage reflection about it. Multiple examples will suggest multiple lines of reflection that may be relevant.

The remainder of this chapter consists partly in examples of practical Christian thinking and partly in discussing how it can be encouraged at local and denominational levels. Instead of discussing one example in depth, I have chosen to schematize several in order to illustrate the variety of ways practical Christian thinking can proceed. I will take three from the area of personal and family life.

The Use of Money

As a first example let us consider our use of money. Most of us receive a barrage of requests for gifts to good causes. We tend to become hardened and to throw most of them away, barely considered. But is this Christian?

The biblical teaching about money, especially that of Jesus, is particularly disturbing. Taken straightforwardly, it requires that we give to all those who ask of us as long as we have anything to give. Keeping something for a rainy day is simply not part of his instruction. Still more difficult would it be to justify the accumulation of capital for investment.

With very few exceptions contemporary Christians have either ignored Jesus' teaching on possessions or found ways around it. We neither give away all our possessions nor encourage others to do so. Yet we cannot go so far as simply to exclude our acquisition and use of possessions from practical Christian thinking. What are some possible Christian reflections?

One may argue, first, that the extreme teachings of Jesus were relevant only in specific circumstances. For example, if one wanted actually to follow the historical Jesus, one had to disencumber oneself of all possessions. But for those who now live in the modern world of business and professions, the rule remains that of the Old Testament—a tithe of one's income.

One may argue, secondly, that Christians are free from all such laws. We should be guided instead by the Spirit, giving spontaneously and freely as we are inwardly moved to do so, not calculating the percentage in an arithmetical way. For some, this will mean much more than 10 percent; for others, less.

One may argue, third, that what is important is nonattachment to possessions. If one is called to a course of action that endangers or exposes one's possessions and refuses the call, that makes clear that one is unacceptably attached. But if one's vocation is compatible with considerable wealth, there is no harm in the latter.

One may argue, fourth, that the crucial point is that we seek first the realm of God. That may mean many things in practice. But at least it means that we will order our lives to ends that are not self-serving. When we do so, our possessions, as well as our persons, will subserve that end. We will not earn money in order to increase our possessions but in order to accomplish the ends toward which we find ourselves, as Christians, called to work.

To simplify this reflection I have abstracted from responsibilities to family members. Let us consider the issues as faced by a single person assumed to be without family obligations. Are all of these options valid for Christians? Are all equally valid?

In my judgment the first fails theologically. Jesus' teaching cannot be dismissed as having only occasional relevance. It supersedes for Christians the legalistic rule of tithing. For Christians the legalistic rule cannot supersede Jesus. But this does not mean that tithing should be discouraged. It is an excellent discipline. It keeps before one the point that as a Christian one is steward of one's possessions rather than owner. And it provides needed funds for the church and other worthy causes. It allows one to budget in such a way that one can respond positively to some of the worthy requests that pour in.

The second response escapes the legalism of the first, but it comes close to antinomianism. Freedom from the law is not to be equated with sheer spontaneity. One can indeed argue, with Augustine, that if we love God, we can do what we please. But that is because what we please is then ordered to the love of God. That is different from what is usually meant by spontaneity. It fits better into some of the latter options.

Some spontaneity in responding to the many appeals we receive is desirable, but by itself it cannot be *the* Christian norm.

The third option is correct as far as it goes. The issue *is* attachment. But our attachment is not shown only by refusing a call to a new job. It is also shown by holding onto our goods when others need them worse than we do. The formulation above is too likely to be a rationalization for self-indulgence. It focuses too much on the spiritual condition of the one who possesses and too little on the real needs of others.

The fourth position is the most appropriate response to Jesus' teaching in changed circumstances. It is the option involved in the vow of poverty taken by Catholic monastics. By abandoning all worldly possessions they can give themselves wholly to their spiritual calling. But that depends on institutional support that enables one to leave all money matters to others. It is also the option followed by leading Reformers. The examples of Luther and Wesley are instructive. Considerable funds passed through their hands, and neither gave simply to any who asked, but both used their funds for purposes that transcended themselves. Neither accumulated wealth.

A contemporary movement that offers an analogous fullness of Christian response to Jesus' teaching is the New Road Map Foundation. It helps people reflect on their priorities and then plan their lives so as to realize these. This means subordinating the making and spending of money to other ends, usually ends of service. Some persons work until they have enough savings so that they can expect to live—frugally—on the income from these savings. They then spend the remainder of their lives in volunteer service. They do not give to all who ask, but they do order their lives to the realm of God.

Of course, there are other people who do not need to retire in order to give themselves to the causes in which they most believe. One may be paid to serve in such a way. For some ministers this works well. But we ministers are almost as likely as others to enjoy the acquisition of money as an independent end that affects our commitment to service. All too often we measure our success by the salaries we receive.

I have argued that the fourth option is the fullest response to Jesus' teaching and the most Christian one. But I abstracted from family responsibilities in supporting it. In the real world, matters are never this simple. Most of us, during much of our lives, do have family obligations. Fulfilling these is a part of a responsible Christian life. The tension between fulfilling the desires of members of families and meeting the more urgent needs of others is one with which most Christians must live. For many, some self-imposed rule, such as tithing, is the most practical solution.

A Problem in Parenting

Let us take as a second example a typical problem that can arise in contemporary parenting. We are assuming that the parents want to act as Christians. Let us suppose that the question is whether to allow their sixteen-year-old son to take the family car and drive his date to a dance in a neighboring town. It would be his first chance to do so. He is a good driver, the parents think well of the girl, and they are glad for him to go to the dance. Their only concern is about drinking.

No alcohol will be served at the dance, which will be well chaperoned, but some of the older boys will probably bring liquor in their cars, and there is likely to be drinking in the adjacent parking lot. The son has not drunk much, but he is susceptible to peer pressure and especially from boys a bit older. For him the objection to the drinking of minors and even to driving while under the influence function more as adult rules, obeyed to avoid punishment, than as internalized principles of personal safety and well-being. His girlfriend is too young to drive, so that even if he does drink, he will drive home.

What are the alternatives for the parents? Consider three standard options.

First, they can simply refuse permission on the grounds that they cannot trust their son not to drink. They will make clear that he is permitted to drive to parties where there is no danger of his drinking alcohol and that, if and when he demonstrates that he is immune to the temptation to drink, the restriction will be removed. They can offer to drive him to the party and come for him as they did before he received his driving license.

Second, they can explain their great concern about this matter and the consequences that will follow if he drinks, pointing out the temptation he is likely to experience. They can remind him of the responsibility he has for the safety of his date and how much his own well-being matters to his parents. After this, they can leave the final decision to him. This will communicate their concern and press him toward taking responsibility for his own actions.

Third, they can have an open discussion with their son explaining their concerns and trying to work out together an arrangement that would meet his needs to be grown-up while limiting the risk. For example, the discussion might generate the idea of a double date with a couple who will not be driving themselves, but one of whom could drive home if the son should drink.

Any of these courses of action can be defended as Christian. But they express different views of what it means to be a Christian and, specifically, different views of God. The first fits best with an authoritarian model of Christianity. If God is the all-controlling, benevolent lawgiver who orders all things for our well-being, then it can easily follow that parents should be all-controlling, benevolent lawgivers for their children. The rules should be clear. In this case the rule is that the son cannot drive the car to a place where alcohol will be available until he has demonstrated his ability to resist peer pressure to drink. The son will learn that he lives in a world of rules and a world where decisions are made for him according to those rules. He may accept them or rebel against them, just as generations of Christians have accepted God's rules or rebelled against them.

The second option shifts the final decision from the parents to the son. The parents try to make sure the son will consider the matter carefully before deciding. But when they have done what they can, they step aside. The son will make the decision and bear the consequences. This corresponds with a different theological vision—one of a universe of freedom rather than of law. The son learns that he decides, that decisions are not made for him. He learns the anguish and terror of decision and the responsibility that accompanies it. This fits well with the theological views of Christian existentialists.

The third option moves toward a shared decision. The son is not left to decide alone, but neither is the decision made for him. The decision arises out of a conversation and is one for which both parents and son take responsibility. The goal is to find a solution that both meets the needs and desires of the son and also protects against the greatest dangers that are involved. We may suppose that several ideas are tried out before a consensus is reached. The son is learning to make decisions and to take responsibility for them, but he is not experiencing the anguish and terror that are felt in isolation. If the decision turns out not to have been a good one, his parents will share responsibility with him. This fits with an understanding of person-in-community, where the community may be thought to include God. In this view, Christian life does not consist as much in either/or decisions by individuals as in working together with the expectation that God guides us through that process.

This example depicts a situation in which there are multiple options. My discussion has been limited to showing how different types of response are correlated with different views of how God acts in the world. My own views are closest to the third option. I believe that God works in and through open discussion and that through it possibilities not previously considered can emerge. Most decisions are not either/or choices between just two options, such as obedience and disobedience. I also believe that we exist in community and share one another's burdens. But the point here is not to argue for a particular theological view and its practical concomitant. It is to show how our practical Christian judgments can reflect our beliefs about God.

A Family Crisis

There are other situations in which an either/or choice cannot be avoided. There the task of deciding as Christians takes on a different form. Consider the situation of an unmarried fifteen-year-old girl who has become pregnant. Neither she nor her boyfriend is ready for marriage, and all agree that it would be a disaster both for them and for the child. The parents are open to discussing the alternatives with their daughter and working toward a shared decision.

At this point, no one except the boyfriend and the members of the girl's immediate family know about the pregnancy. An abortion can be arranged legally that is quite safe and confidential. The girl can continue with her life little changed, except that she is determined not to let this happen to her again. For the parents, also, this is the easy and comfortable solution. For the daughter to carry the fetus to term and then to keep the child would be a source of embarrassment to all and a serious limitation on the girl's prospects for employment and marriage. In any case, she does not have the maturity necessary to be a good mother. To give up the child for adoption would be emotionally painful after attachments were formed, even though it would have fewer adverse effects in other ways. At this point the frightened girl has not developed an attachment to the fetus, and she would like, above all else, to return to her life as it was before the pregnancy. For the girl, for the boyfriend, and for the girl's family, abortion seems the best solution.

But the family wants to act responsibly as Christians. Does that change the considerations? Is abortion a sin, even the especially heinous sin of murder? If so, of course, the Christian decision must be for the girl and her family to make whatever sacrifices are required to bring the fetus to term. The decision as to whether to raise the child or to put it up for adoption is secondary.

How are they to decide? One step may be to consult their pastor or someone else whose judgments they trust about what is Christian. But at some point they will have to come to their own decision as to whether abortion is, in principle, a sin, whether it is the killing of a human being.

Obviously, this family would not consider killing a child or an adult even to save themselves great embarrassment and extreme difficulties. Hence, if they are persuaded that the fetus is a human person, in the sense in which children and adults are human persons, they will not abort the fetus. The issue seems straightforward. But the decision as to whether the fetus is a human being is not so easy to make.

It turns out that the first major divide in the debate on this issue is a philosophical one. That does not reduce the importance of thinking about it as Christians. But the decision on a philosophical issue requires attention to philosophical arguments that cannot be settled simply by appeal to Christian beliefs. To be a Christian in this area is to try to check one's biases and think as clearly as possible.

The philosophical question one quickly encounters is this: is there an "essence" of being human, such that the fertilized ovum and the fetus must be, at any given stage, either a human being or not? Or should we think of a long process of becoming human that is not completed until after birth?

If the family decides for the "essentialist" position, namely, that at each stage of development the fetus either is or is not a human being, then a second question arises. At what point does the ovum become a human being? Is the fertilized egg already a human being? If so, abortion is always murder. Is a functioning brain required in order that a human being be present? In that case it will be important to perform the abortion immediately to obviate the chances that a human being is being killed. Or does the fetus become a human being only when it is viable? In that case there is not the same rush.

Alternatively, the family may take the side of process thought. In this case there is no one point at which what was previously not a human being at all abruptly becomes one. There is a potentiality for becoming a human being that is progressively actualized. Even the unfertilized egg has the potential to become a human being. The newborn infant is still not a full human being. In between it is a matter of degree. To destroy a fetus in the first trimester is certainly not murder, but it is feticide, and that too must be taken seriously.

The earlier the killing the less weighty do the reasons need to be. This is because what is killed has less intrinsic importance and because others, especially the mother, are less attached. Devices that prevent conception or the implantation of the fertilized ovum need little justification. The killing of a viable fetus needs a very great deal. In the example we are considering, the disruption of the girl's life and of that of her family would be likely to outweigh the evil of the abortion, if this is carried out quite early in the pregnancy. But if they wait until the fetus becomes active and the girl becomes conscious of its partly independent existence, the scales may tip in the opposite direction.

I have presented the options here as philosophical, whereas those in the parenting example were more explicitly correlated with theological ideas of God. This is ironic, since abortion issues are often regarded as theological, whereas parenting issues are typically thought of as primarily psychological. The reason for the belief that abortion issues are theological is that the Western church long ago wedded itself to a particular philosophical position—natural law theory. Although this was not continued by the Reformers, much of its spirit has remained alive among Protestants as well.

However, there is a theological component as well. The horror of killing is heightened by the emphasis on God's love of all human beings and especially the poor and powerless. Christians have been consistent in opposing infanticide because of their conviction that we should follow God in special concern for the powerless, among which the newborn infant is a clear and compelling case. The early church extended this concern for the powerless back into the womb. Still, its concern was for powerless human beings, and until recently its greatest teachers did not extend the status of being human back to the early weeks of pregnancy.

Today we realize that the church's historic teaching focused on the fetus at the expense of the woman. The patriarchal character of traditional theology is overwhelming, and it is clearly manifest in these discussions. Men make the rules and apply them with very little attention to their effects on women or to women's experience in general. The gospel, on the other hand, liberates women and empowers them. The prohibition of abortion by the male-dominated church continues the disempowerment of women and the neglect of their point of view. All this is also a relevant consideration for the Christian family of our example.

These more explicitly Christian considerations intensify the anguish of the decision: one heightens the claims of the fetus for consideration, the other intensifies the importance of not destroying the prospects of the girl. My own judgment is that they do not finally alter the decision based on how we understand the process of the fetus becoming a human being. Women's experience does not lead to supporting the killing of powerless human beings even if that facilitates fuller realization of the woman's own potentials. On the other hand, God's special care for powerless human beings does not tell us when a fertilized ovum becomes one of those powerless human beings for whom God has special care.

The Norms of Practical Christian Thinking

I have proposed three topics for practical Christian thinking. The type of reflection they elicit in the course of practical Christian thinking is quite diverse. In the case of the use of money, reference was to the teachings of Jesus. In the discussion of parenting, appeal was to basic Christian understanding of God's relation to the world. With regard to abortion, the critical issue was philosophical. In each of these cases, it would be legitimate for a critic to demand justification for the direction taken. It would also be possible to propose other lines of reflection as equally or more appropriate for practical Christian thinking on these issues.

Nevertheless, the choices made were not arbitrary, and the three types of consideration illustrate a wide range of practical Christian thinking. With regard to money, there is a great deal of biblical teaching as there is not in the other two instances. A survey of all biblical teaching about money would be appropriate, but for Christians Jesus is particularly authoritative. On the other hand, here as elsewhere we cannot simply take Jesus' teachings in an unqualified way as providing the rules by which to live. On this matter we have much to learn from the history of Christianity and the varied ways in which Christians have wrestled with the extremeness and impracticality in most contexts of direct application of Jesus' teachings. We must look for ways in our changed context to apply to ourselves the deeper intention we discern in Jesus' message. I propose that we understand this deeper intention as placing service to God and to fellow human beings as primary and subordinating our relationship to money to this goal. This approach is applicable to a wide range of practical issues.

On the other hand, it is not so directly relevant to particular issues that arise in parenting. Gaining guidance from Jesus in particular or the Bible in general on how to make the kind of decision with which the second example dealt is a far more indirect matter. The issue has to do with how best to exercise authority over one who is clearly subject to that authority. We can then study the Bible as a whole, and Jesus in particular, to see how authority is best exercised. This could be a complex task, but we would certainly conclude that authority is exercised for the sake of those over whom it is exercised. Hence the primary consideration is what is best for the son and, of course, for others who would be affected by the son's actions. Within that context we can look to the Bible for images of how authority is best exercised for the sake of the other. We can ask how Jesus exercises authority, and how, if he reveals God's nature, we are to think of God's exercise of authority.

Of course, we cannot act just as God acts, and absurd conclusions could be drawn from too rigidly following such patterns. But in some important sense we are to be perfect as God is perfect; our love for others is to reflect and respond to God's love for us; and we are to forgive others as God forgives us. It is natural and proper to seek to be, in some limited way, like that which we worship. Since Jesus' basic image for God is parental, parental issues are among those in which this modeling of our actions toward those placed in our care on those of God toward us makes most sense.

Hence, how we think of God and God's relation to us is highly relevant to our practical Christian thinking. In this and many other ways practical Christian thinking turns us toward central issues in traditional theology. We cannot separate requires our practical concerns from basic theoretical ones. Chapter 4 will return to this question.

In dealing with both money and parenting, much of the relevant consideration requires reference to extra-biblical matters. We must think about what is possible in our actual circumstances and to what needs we can effectively minister in order to establish a Christian policy toward money. We cannot get the answers to such questions from the Bible. We must consider the level of maturity reached by the boy and the likelihood of temptation at the party, when deciding what to allow him to do. We cannot learn such matters from the Bible. Nevertheless, in both these instances, in quite different ways, the decisive norms are biblical, and once the factual information is available, the biblical norms can be acted on.

This is not always the situation. It is important to realize that there are many considerations relevant to practical Christian thinking that are not factual in any simple sense and yet are not to be settled by appeal to the Bible. The third example above illustrated this. There are factual matters about the girl's condition, the prospects of marriage, the preferences of the boyfriend, and so forth. And there is the biblical requirement that the parents act in love toward all who are involved. It is also clear that murder is a peculiarly drastic violation of the law of love, and that much sacrifice on the part of others is preferable to committing murder.

What we cannot learn from the Bible is whether the abortion of a fetus is murder. The topic is not discussed. In the only passage that comes close, Exodus 21:22ff., the indication is that killing a fetus is not murder. But even those who are extremely biblicist in their use of texts are not likely to consider this decisive for Christians. The question of how to think of the fetus requires a quite different kind of reflection from Bible study. I have called it philosophical.

Philosophical ideas have played an enormous role, for good and ill, in the history of Christian practical thinking.

They do so today. Since there are alternative philosophies, the choice among them for the Christian finally involves their compatibility and suitability with the Christian faith. My own judgment is that process thinking is more helpful for Christians than essentialist thinking, and this would lead me to favor abortion in the preceding story. But it is important for Christians to recognize the difficulty and uncertainty of such decisions about philosophical issues and to respect those who differ.

This discussion, combined with the examples themselves, should suffice to indicate that there is no one pattern or rule as to how practical Christian thinking proceeds in all cases. It should also show that such thinking, though demanding, is possible for all Christians. Theology as practical Christian thinking is not hopelessly obscure, complex, or esoteric.

Support Groups for Practical Christian Thinking

There is no assurance that individual Christians will think well when they try to think as Christians. There is no assurance that I have done so. The test is the quality of the reflection, and we are not good judges of our own work. The fact that each situation requires a different type of reflection means that no recipes are available. The church cannot teach people *how* to engage in practical Christian thinking, although it can do much more than it now does to encourage such reflection and to suggest patterns it may follow.

What the church *can* do best is to provide opportunities for people to learn to think practically as Christians by doing so in a context of supportive, yet critical, Christian friends. It would be nice to think that ordinary church life already provided this context, but we know that it rarely does. Hence, the most practical proposal I am making in this chapter on practical Christian thinking is that congregations organize support groups of Christians who want to learn how to think better as Christians about the decisions they face in daily life.

Such support groups can come about in two ways. One is by the modification of an existing group. The other is by starting one primarily for this purpose.

One type of existing support group works primarily with people's feelings. It performs an admirable Christian service by helping persons experience the assurance that others care for them. Sometimes it enables people to talk frankly about their feelings for the first time. It would be ideal for groups of this sort, where mutual openness is already well established, to take on the additional role of reflecting together explicitly as Christians about the decisions its members face. They would be unlikely to confuse Christian decisions with legalistic ones.

Another type of existing group focuses on Bible study. These groups already engage in some of the discussion for which I am calling. It would not be hard to give a larger place to practical Christian thinking. The danger is that there would be too much effort to find solutions to problems directly in the Bible. But since the Bible itself warns against that kind of approach, this danger is not inevitable.

The second approach is to create new support groups among those who are directly attracted by the project of learning to think practically as Christians. In this case it would be important to spend sufficient time developing mutual understanding and affection so that problems are not dealt with in abstraction from the real people involved. But that is likely to happen in any case as a by-product of the shared task.

However the group is formed, the primary work, at least initially, can be sharing what those in the group already know and have experienced. For example, I could share where my practical Christian thinking has led me on one of the examples above, and others could react supportively but critically. No doubt I would then see alternatives I have missed, ones that are better than those I have advocated.

People should not be intimidated from joining by the fear that scholarly study is required. But as time goes by, the members may see that they could think better as Christians about some of the issues that concern them if they knew more about Scripture or tradition or psychology or the wider social context. At that point some members can begin studying and sharing what they find. Some scholarly work in history and theology that now seems remote and irrelevant would turn out to be quite pertinent and even exciting. But even if this does not happen, mutual critical support in thinking as Christians will lead to greater Christian maturity.

Practical Christian Thinking for the Congregation

Thus far I have considered problems that arise in personal and family life and what it means to think about them in an intentionally Christian way. But practical problems also arise at other levels. Local churches have structures through which they make decisions about their corporate lives. The discussions that lead to the decisive votes are rarely good examples of practical Christian thinking. Yet we should not be cynical. Most of these decisions are about implementing established goals. It would often be distorting to claim particular Christian reasons for the means adopted.

Occasionally there is an impassioned speech arguing that some particular program *must* be adopted because the Christian faith requires it. Sometimes that raises sights and reminds people what they are doing as Christians. But making absolute claims can distort the planning process. Often the Christian character of the business meeting is expressed more in avoiding the introduction of absolutes and allowing all voices to be heard in the process of reaching as much consensus as possible. One need not make explicit reference to Christian faith in implementing that kind of group process.

On the other hand, many congregations do sense the need to reflect as Christians on what they are doing. Sometimes they have planning retreats or special sessions devoted to defining their mission. These provide contexts for practical Christian thinking.

On most of these occasions, the practical Christian thinking does not go very far. If there is general satisfaction with
what is happening in the church, the result is likely to be
that participants remind themselves of why they are doing
what they are doing. Usually this reminding is in fairly general terms that can be understood quite variously by those
who accept them.

Only when the basic ongoing program of the church is
challenged by proposals for change is the context established
for more serious practical Christian thinking. This can happen when a growing congregation is ready to build a sanctuary. A diversity of views as to what a sanctuary should be like
may surface, reflecting different views of worship. Or if an
inner-city church with a suburban congregation considers
transforming its physical plant into a center for service to its
neighbors, real issues about the nature and mission of that
congregation will surface. Or if a charismatic group develops
within a congregation and seeks to influence the larger church,
fundamental questions about Christian experience and about
the Holy Spirit will be raised. If one segment of a congregation proposes that the church declare itself a part of the sanctuary movement or suggests the welcoming of lesbians and
gays, practical Christian thinking will be called for.

The problem is that few congregations are ready to respond well when the occasion for serious Christian thinking
of this sort arises. They have no practice in such thinking.
The missional statements they have written in the absence
of such need for decisions give little guidance. Hence, the
reaction to the proposals tends to express personal emotional
response based on other loyalties rather than considered efforts to decide as Christians. It is difficult to learn how to
engage in practical Christian thinking for the first time in
the heat of controversy.

At present there is no place in the church's organizational
structure for ongoing practical Christian thinking. Yet the
incapacity of the congregation to make its basic decisions on

a reflective Christian basis is a serious threat to the long-term health of the church. Nothing is more important for the renewal of the church than organs for practical Christian thinking.

Above I proposed support groups for church members who want to make their personal decisions as Christians. Such a group might, in time, reflect about the decisions facing the congregation as well. Alternatively, a group could be created specifically for this purpose.

But where can the motivation for such a group be found until it is urgently needed—and is then too late? It must come basically from the desire that the church become more Christian. But it can be stimulated by more specific concerns. For example, in many congregations there are at least a few women who would like to see sexist language removed from the liturgy. Many pastors have taken steps in this direction, and some hymnbooks have been modified. Some of the changes are not problematic. But others have caused heated controversy.

To illustrate, some who are willing to have inclusive language used in reference to people, insist that references to God employ the masculine pronoun. Others who are willing to avoid the masculine pronoun in general references to God, still insist that the first two persons of the Trinity always be named Father and Son. Since the congregation has some control over its own liturgy, a group could study the issues involved, engage in its own practical Christian thinking, and discuss its conclusions with the pastor.

In many congregations there is at least latent tension between different views of what should happen to children in the early grades of church school or in a church-sponsored kindergarten. Some believe that it is important for the children to memorize Bible verses and learn Bible stories even if they do not understand them. Others believe that what the children need is the experience of being loved and the opportunity to explore their world in a context that points to

God as the source and full embodiment of love. Of course, these approaches are not wholly irreconcilable, but they do suggest different views of what the church should be about. The issues involved here could be clarified, and practical Christian thinking could lead to fresh proposals.

In many congregations there are not only different positions on political issues but also different views of whether and how the church should relate to these matters. These differences would provide another area for practical Christian thinking. Further, a group organized to consider these questions could then proceed to consider some of the political issues themselves *as Christians*, checking their tendencies to make their political judgments on other grounds. They might decide that the church's role is more to teach its members how to think *as Christians* about these matters than to take positions as a church. On the other hand, there might be some issues on which they would decide that the Christian position is so clear that the church *should* speak out.

I hope I have given enough examples of topics that such a group could address to overcome any sense of its irrelevance. The group would have, of course, only moral authority, and it would gain that only gradually. But if it did its work well, it would change the climate of the congregation and the way decisions are made. It could become proactive, making suggestions to the church of directions it should take, even quite radical ones, and it would be taken seriously as others were convinced that the proposals reflected genuinely Christian practical thinking. Of course, this would not be likely to happen if the group's membership consisted in representatives of only one faction within a divided church.

Regional and national judicatories often know in advance some of the major issues that they will be facing. They make this information available to delegates who will share in making decisions. At present these delegates rarely receive much help from their congregations in thinking about these matters. If a group existed in the church dedicated to considering such questions from a Christian perspective, the cause of Christ at many levels would be advanced.

There is still another range of tasks or topics. One of the scandals of the American church is its failure to pay attention to conciliar statements. Few American Christians know what position the National Council of Churches or the World Council of Churches has taken until they read a hostile article in *Reader's Digest*. Much less do they know anything about the reasoning that goes into it. Often, before adopting a position, the Councils will send proposals to the member churches for their study. But rare indeed is the local church that takes part in that study. For a local congregation, or a responsible study group within it, to interact reflectively with the conciliar movements would be a rich experience for both.

A local church group undertaking to play this role for the congregation would have to be committed to study in a way the group recommended above would not. It is eminently desirable that individual Christians think more deeply and clearly about the relevance of their faith for their daily life. Supporting one another in that enterprise will both foster this thinking and improve its quality. The further gains that could come from study are desirable, but their absence will not invalidate what is already gained.

But a group that is asked to advise the church takes on a corporate responsibility that cannot be fulfilled merely by the mutual interaction of its thoughtful members. Furthermore, the issues it is asked to address have added dimensions. Thoughtful Christians should not be intimidated by the complexity of their task, but it should not be concealed from them.

For example, consider the matter of sexist language in reference to the persons of the Trinity. Must the first person be called Father and the second, Son, despite the continuation of patriarchal language that entails?

To understand the force of the objection, at least some members must have more than passing acquaintance with the feminist literature, and especially the theological and anti-theological feminist literature. But also, in order to understand the force of the resistance to change, one must know something of the history of the doctrine of the Trinity and its role in the church. Since the Trinitarian formulation is especially connected with baptism, the importance of baptism in ecumenical church life must be understood. This range of knowledge cannot be taken for granted in even an elite group of laywomen and men in the average congregation.

Even this can be only the beginning. Very basic questions of the understanding of "God" have to be considered. Does the word *God* have ontological reference? If so, is there any sense in which gender applies to this referent? If not, is there any reason that symbols for this God should be masculine rather than feminine? For example, are the characteristics of God or the way that God relates to the world more like a father than like a mother?

Are we bound in any way by the fact that Jesus addressed God as "Father"? Is the reference to "Son" in the Trinitarian formula a reference to Jesus or to the everlasting divine reality that was incarnate in him? If the latter, could Word or Wisdom be substituted for Son without loss?

I will not proceed with the questions. No one has yet sorted all this out, and clearly there will never be just one way of doing so. We cannot ask our lay study group to resolve the problem for the ecumenical church! But that does not mean that it cannot advise its own pastor and worship committee and involve a larger portion of the church in reflecting on the issues.

My own view is that for the present we must continue to use the language of Father, Son, and Holy Spirit when we baptize to ensure that the validity of baptism in each congregation is accepted by the ecumenical church. Similarly, I would retain "Father" in the Lord's Prayer. And I would not change the wording of the ecumenical creeds.

To balance these concessions to tradition, made for the sake of ecumenical unity, it may be possible to introduce explicitly feminine imagery at enough other places to overcome the heavily patriarchal character of the liturgy. Most references to the Trinity can use nonsexist language. Even on the occasion of baptism it may be possible to baptize "in the name of the One who is Mother and Father of us all, and of the divine Wisdom who came to us as the Son." These are the best compromises I can come up with at present. Whether our hypothetical study group can do better remains to be seen, but it will only be out of wide discussion that the church can move toward a new language that reflects our developing sensibilities.

Practical Christian Thinking for Denominations

In conclusion, let me make a proposal also for Protestant denominations. At present most of them, like congregations, lack any organ for thought. Occasionally, an unusual bureaucrat introduces such an organ inside one of the departments or agencies. From time to time the national judicatory appoints a group to study a particular issue in a sustained way. Occasionally, an existing body, such as the Council of Bishops of the United Methodist Church, undertakes to guide the church's thinking on an urgent issue. But overall, the fact remains that the denominations have no organ for thinking.

For this they pay a high price. Whereas we Christians believe that Christ is the Light of the world, that in our faith we have a fundamental understanding of reality that is profoundly illuminating, we have no way to articulate this and share it with the world except individually. The productions of *ad hoc* committees cannot compete in the marketplace of ideas. Hence, in this country the wider public does not look to the Protestant churches for guidance on important questions, and fewer and fewer church members do so either.

On the other hand, the Protestant churches have never employed a larger number of scholars. I refer to the faculties of the schools of theology. These faculties produce a substantial array of literature, much of it impressive, but very little of it directly relates to the issues on which the church needs guidance and on which it is called to speak to the world. In any case, what they write is taken simply as the expression of the private opinions of individual scholars. They are not authorized to speak for the church.

My suggestion is that the church employ the seminaries as organs of practical Christian thinking. This would not mean, of course, that the publications of individual faculty members would have official status as church documents. But the denomination would ask individual faculties collectively to study topics of importance for the church and to provide guidance to the church in their resolution. This guidance might still be ignored or, after serious consideration, rejected. But the work of the church's best scholars would be directed to issues with which the church must deal; and at least at times it would be taken seriously and have its influence.

I suspect the main reason the church does not make use of its faculties is suspicion. It is afraid, with some justification, that its scholars view the world differently from most of its pastors and laypeople. Some members of its faculties are post-Christian, and others are alienated from the local church. Their reports, therefore, would be controversial.

The problems are real. Church leadership and seminary faculties have long been drifting apart. Mutual suspicions are extensive and, in part, warranted. But the way to bridge the gulf is not by widening it. It is by asking for help on points where seminary faculties are better able to provide it than are any other agencies within the church.

Once a crisis develops in a denomination, seminary faculties are not in a position to resolve it. Academicians are not geared that way. But if twenty years ago the denominations had asked some of their faculties to study the Christian response to the sexual revolution, by the time the issues surrounding homosexuality forced themselves on the churches' attention, there would have been a thoughtful body of practical Christian thinking on which to draw. If even today the denominations would ask some of their seminaries to study the issues surrounding suicide, euthanasia, and death with dignity, they could give leadership on these issues instead of waiting for attention in the public media to force them to come up with theologically questionable statements. Even more important would be studies on economic life and the relation of the church to that. The relation of church and state needs study. Ecological issues, the rights of animals, the right stance toward Judaism, the relation of witness and dialogue, and the issue of language about God discussed above are all appropriate topics for sustained inquiry and advice to the church. There are many others.

Perhaps not all seminaries would accept this role. Some faculty members are so immersed in their own guilds that they would not know how to speak to the issues arising in the church and the world. But enough would respond, and respond well, to change the character of the church's thinking. It could also change the character of the seminaries and alter their inner relation to the church in ways that would benefit the students as well.

This chapter has been about practical Christian thinking. It is also an exercise in practical Christian thinking. It has taken as its problem the lack of good practical Christian thinking in the churches and has proposed ways in which this could be increased, improved, and made more influential. This is an area in which major improvements could be effected at quite minor costs. Whether it would result in church growth cannot be foretold, but a church that thought would cease to be decadent. It is worth a try.

Theology
as the
Criticism
of
Assumptions

Reflection About Vocations

Practical Christian thinking usually connotes the sort of thinking dealt with in Chapter 2. This relates quite directly to the personal and family life of the Christian or to the problems faced by the church. These problems lead to interest in social issues as well, particularly those that become politically important in our nation. But practical Christian thinking is needed in other fields as well.

One extension of practical Christian thinking that touches the lives of many Christians is reflection about their work. Some young people think seriously as Christians about their calling. Others reconsider their vocation in midlife and select a second career. Often Christians are drawn to the service professions, such as teaching, social work, health care, and especially professional ministry within the church itself.

These seem to give more direct expression to Christian concern for the well-being of others than does the world of business and industry. But in fact some of the products of business and industry are equally essential to human well-being. The decision as to what one is called to do is complex. The church could be more helpful to its members as they reflect about their vocations.

Whatever line of work one enters, other questions arise as one tries to carry out one's responsibilities on the job. Some of these questions cut across occupations. For example, most jobs involve interpersonal relations; and how we treat other people, whether only as means to our ends or truly as ends in themselves, is a fundamental issue for everyone. Sometimes there is a tension between treating another person as an end and advancing the business or institution one serves.

There are also special problems and issues raised within each type of job. If one is engaged in manufacturing, one may decide that the product is harmful to people. If so, should one quit? In most cases, quitting would not affect the quantity of the harmful substance that is produced, and it would cause hardship to oneself and one's family. On the other hand, it is hard to understand one's Christian vocation as being the production of goods the world would be better off without.

Recently this issue has focused on certain types of armaments. Some Christians left their jobs rather than continue to produce nuclear weapons whose abundance already threatened the future of humanity. Many others, of course, kept their jobs because the cost to the family of giving them up was too high. The church could be more helpful in such crises of the Christian conscience.

At some times and places the church has recognized the need to help laypeople think about their workaday lives from a Christian point of view. Especially in West Germany after World War II lay academies flourished. Factory workers met to reflect as Christians about their work as laborers. Business people, lawyers, doctors, and teachers also did so.

Some such reflection took place in this country as well. The example with which I am most familiar was the Faculty Christian Fellowship. This consisted of Christian teachers in colleges and universities. Their purpose was to consider their responsibilities as professors in the context of secular higher education. Could or should their faith make a difference in the classroom? Certainly it would express itself in keen personal concern for the students.

But should faith affect teaching in any other way? One view was that it should motivate the teacher to do the best job possible, but that the job to be done would not differ from that of any other good teacher of the same subjects. Others argued that Christian teachers should share their faith in whatever ways the restrictions of a secular context allowed.

The debate typically focused on the issue of whether the material to be taught is objective. If so, then there is little room for expressing one's faith directly in its presentation. On the other hand, if the material is always interpreted from some point of view, then why should the Christian point of view be excluded? For example, if Christians consider important certain developments in European history that secular historians neglect, should not the Christian professor of history be free to present the material in a way that displays that importance?

This was a valuable discussion. Some of it has been carried on in other contexts. But as a separate program for Christian faculty it faded in the 1960s at the same time that more and more universities took up the teaching of religion and even established departments for this purpose. The issue of objectivity focused instead on the teaching of religion itself.

The discussion in departments of religion was skewed by their particular circumstances. Their members knew that they were viewed skeptically by many other faculty, who suspected that religion departments would be centers of moral exhortation and religious propaganda rather than genuine participants in the academic quest. In response, teachers of religion leaned over backward to avoid letting their teaching be influenced by their personal religious beliefs. Accordingly, the ideal of objectivity triumphed, and the kinds of questions central to the Faculty Christian Fellowship faded into the background. They are now coming back under different auspices, especially that of liberationists. But there is not yet a serious revival of discussion among Christian faculty members about their distinctive role and task.

Today the only area in which Christians are vigorously discussing how people should act in their professional lives seems to be in medicine. As medical science advances, new issues arise not covered by established professional ethics. For example, with increasing ability to save lives by transplanting organs, doctors face new questions. There are more people who need transplants than there are available organs. How should doctors decide whose lives to save?

Also, doctors can now keep alive for many years the bodies of persons whose higher faculties are irretrievably lost. Is it right to do so? Or should these people, as human beings, be considered dead, and their bodies also allowed to die? Should these bodies be considered sources of organs for transplanting to others in whom they would contribute to a valuable human life? When is one dealing with a human being, when, not? Theologians and Christian ethicists are often involved in hospital committees dealing with such issues.

Sometimes Christian business and professional people have gathered to discuss the ethical issues they confront in their work. But the church at local or denominational levels could take far more initiative than it does on such matters. This would not mean that groups of Christian business executives or lawyers would be lectured to by preachers or theologians. It is Christian executives and lawyers who are best equipped to help one another, but if the assistance of theologians or pastors is wanted, this should be given. Laypeople should be able to expect support from the church as they reflect on their calling.

Critique of Institutions
Practical Christian thinking about work often takes the institutional context for granted. For example, professors can take their colleges and universities for granted and simply ask how they, as Christians, should function in this context. This was the focus of the previous section. But as Christians see how restrictive such a context is, they may also raise fundamental questions about the institution that imposes these restrictions. For example, why should there be institutions of higher education at all, and if they are needed, what is their proper function and role in society? What changes are needed if they are to fulfill their true calling?

The institution Christians in general know best is the church. It is appropriate that this also be the institution we criticize most severely. And this has, indeed, been the case. Throughout the Middle Ages there were repeated protests that the church, instead of being the servant of the people, exploited them for the sake of its own wealth and power. The church had sufficient power to suppress these movements, for the most part, but they came to expression in Francis of Assisi in a way with which the church had to come to terms. Following Francis' death there was a long struggle between those Franciscans who maintained his radical vision and those who were prepared to share in the more common forms of church life. The Lutheran Reformation was precipitated in part by protest against the way the Papacy was exploiting popular piety to raise money for St. Peter's cathedral, a crowning symbol of the might and wealth of the church.

Another long-standing criticism of the church as institution has been its alliance, since Constantine, with political authority. In Western Europe this became more extreme in Protestantism, where the counterpoint of the Papacy was removed. Sectarian and free church forms of Protestantism insisted on independence of the church from the state, often at considerable cost.

Some of these sectarian and free church groups also protested the structure of power within the churches themselves. This was characteristically hierarchical. In most churches clergy had assumed power and privilege, and laity had been assigned second-class status. Democratic rule within the church was demanded, and to some extent actually achieved in congregationally governed bodies.

Unfortunately, even democratically ruled churches are often subject to legitimate criticism. One of the most searching of such criticisms in the United States has been that most white Protestant churches assented to racism, if they did not actively support it. This racism was directed especially at blacks. This criticism, too, has been heard, and most churches have tried, with varying degrees of success, to reform.

Recently we have recognized that an equally pervasive failure of the church has been to ignore Paul's teaching that in Christ there is neither male nor female. Even in democratic churches, males have ruled over females. Few churches have yet attained full participation of all laypeople on a truly equal basis, but the ideal is now widely held and functions as the basis for reforms.

During the late nineteenth and early twentieth centuries the Protestant churches engaged in a massive program of evangelistic missions especially in Asia and Africa. This evoked Christian commitment and even sacrifice of a high order. It represents one of the high points of church history. Yet during the twentieth century Christians have come to recognize how closely this Protestant mission was tied to Euro-American colonialism. This repeated the mistakes of Catholic missions in Latin America, which were so often part of Spanish and Portuguese colonization. Many churches are now striving to repent and to throw their weight on the side of liberation movements.

I mention these long-standing, and sometimes successful, criticisms of the church as institution, not to develop them here, but to suggest that within the church we have developed criteria, and a habit of mind, that may have wider application. Instead of simply asking how to operate within the church and its established structures and practices, Christians have also asked how the church should be reformed. Similarly, instead of simply asking how they should operate within other institutions, Christians can also ask how these should be reformed.

This is a task primarily for Christian laity whose vocation lies within these institutions. It is they who understand best the assumptions underlying their institutions and how these assumptions work out in practice. It is they who are best able to bring Christian beliefs and values to bear upon these assumptions, criticize them accordingly, and propose reform.

The proposal that Christians reflect about institutions is not wholly new. Prior to the Reformation, European Christians felt responsibility for all the institutions of society, and they attempted to Christianize them. But since the Reformation, especially in predominantly Protestant countries, this has been less common. The churches have demanded freedom to do their work within essentially secular societies. In exchange, they have let the other institutions do their work on their own terms.

In this country Protestant denominations took the lead in establishing schools, hospitals, and social service agencies. In the nineteenth century Protestant institutions of these types were a major element in American society. They functioned as extensions of the church, institutions through which the church fulfilled much of its mission. But now the situation has changed. Many Protestant institutions remain, but they are a minor factor in a society dominated by tax-supported educational, medical, and social services. Most of the church institutions are only slightly distinguishable from their secular counterparts.

Practical Christian thinking is needed today on two topics. First, there is the question of whether Christian institutions have a distinctive role to play and, if so, what it is. Second, there are basic questions about the nature of the secular institutions. Can Christians affirm them as they stand, or do we have criticisms and proposals for reform that should be introduced into the public debate?

At this point the secularization of church institutions has gone so far that the second question assumes primacy over the first. Only if we as Christians become clearer as to what we think such institutions should be like in general can we also become clearer as to the role those institutions we still influence or control should play. Hence a Christian critique of institutions, their goals and assumptions, is needed.

When the goals of such institutions are formulated very generally, they are noncontroversial. The great majority of Christians favor education, health care, and helping people deal with special problems and crises. But the actual goals of actual institutions are necessarily much more specific. These specific goals shape the way these institutions function, and they are worthy of debate.

For example, should education aim primarily at preparation for jobs, at producing good citizens, at developing personal maturity, at transmitting a cultural tradition, or at something else? Can good education be neutral with regard to competing values emphasized in different religious traditions? Should all children be educated as the majority decides, or should minorities have the opportunity to educate their children in ways they regard as more suitable?

At present our society has decided that the majority should make the decisions with respect to the dominant form of education through high school, that this education should be neutral among competing value claims, that the tradition transmitted will be primarily the secular, nationalist one, and that the function of education should be primarily practical, that is, to prepare people to succeed within contemporary society. Minorities that are dissatisfied with this education are free, within limits, to provide a different education for their children, but they must pay taxes to support the majority education as well.

These decisions have the tacit support of most Protestants. This support developed at a time when Protestant values dominated the public school system, and today it is more on the basis of habit than of renewed reflection in the changing social context. Fresh thinking about the nature and goals of education is urgently needed, and Christians should contribute to this.

The situation is similar with respect to the institutions that serve our health. The dominant institutions are controlled by the medical profession. This profession is geared primarily to dealing with sickness, and it does so chiefly by administering chemicals and by surgery. It is committed to indefinite expansion of ability to overcome diseases. When we are sick or injured, we are all grateful for the remarkable effectiveness of our doctors.

However, there are serious problems with this approach. When treatments that could cure us exist, few people want to forgo them. Yet the cost of providing such treatments to everyone who needs them is prohibitive. The present focus in health care is in principle elitist, in that it provides extraordinary cures for those who can afford them while not being accessible to all.

There are other approaches to health care. There is, first, the focus on preventive medicine. This means both making the environment more healthful and encouraging people to maintain good health through exercise, wholesome eating, and good attitudes. Much of this takes place, but it is peripheral to the primary medical institution in which by far the larger portion of funds is invested. There are also other health care systems, such as homeopathy, chiropractic, and acupuncture, most of which have been excluded from our major institutions.

My point here, again, is that our health care institutions are not beyond critical evaluation. Such evaluation may lead to reaffirmation of support for current institutions in their present form. But it may not. Christian thinking can be an important contribution to such decisions.

It is less necessary to problematize social service institutions, for they are already under critical scrutiny. There are indications that present methods of supporting the poor and aiding in emergencies have created patterns of dependency and irresponsibility. They also require a huge and largely impersonal bureaucracy for their implementation. The results are often dehumanizing. Yet alternatives that meet real human needs effectively are not so easy to propose. There is no question here about the potential fruitfulness of Christian reflection.

I have focused on those institutions with which the church has been most closely associated in the past. But legal institutions are also deserving of criticism. Business and industry require close scrutiny as well, as do communications and recreation.

In no case should we think of ourselves as in position to impose distinctively Christian values on secular institutions. But if our Christian perspective enables us to see problems and propose alternatives that commend themselves to the wider public as well, that can be a significant Christian contribution. Furthermore, we may be in a position to express Christian values through the remaining Christian institutions, thus modeling for the larger society the fruitfulness of an alternative vision.

Critique of the University

Because the secular institution I know the best is the university, I will illustrate the critique of institutions there. The university has taken over from the liberal arts college as the major institution of higher education. Whereas the liberal arts college had a history that rooted it clearly in Christian values, this is much less true of the modern research-oriented university.

The research in question is partly independent of the teaching function of the university. This independent research is determined by what there are funds to pay for rather than by a humanistic or scholarly judgment about what information is needed. In recent decades the largest source of funding has been military-related.

As a locus of teaching, the university is a collection of professional and graduate schools associated with a college. Sometimes the college continues the tradition of liberal arts. More often it is dominated by preprofessional training or preparation for graduate work. Hence, along with unrelated research, it is the professional and graduate schools that establish the ethos of the university.

Within the university, the highest prestige is associated with advanced graduate teaching and the research that accompanies it. This is organized into departments, each of which is committed to the advancement of a particular discipline, such as chemistry, or French literature, or sociology. These disciplines are often divided into subdisciplines that take on considerable autonomy and sometimes achieve separate departmental status. Ideally, every distinguishable subject matter is the object of some discipline.

Each discipline develops methods of approaching its subject matter. Methodological rigor is prized, and education in the department focuses on ensuring that graduates are able to advance the discipline by applying the appropriate method to new problems. As a result they are able to communicate well with one another and to evaluate one another's work. Communication between departments or disciplines is much more difficult, and, in general, academic protocol discourages critical evaluation of work outside one's own field.

The ideals and goals of the university and the assumptions about knowledge that it embodies are all worthy of criticism from a Christian point of view. Christians may appropriately question whether the enormous influence of military research is desirable. Indeed, we may ask whether the university should not make its own judgments about what society really needs rather than have its work determined for it by the availability of funds. Christians cannot ask that Christian values control the direction of university research, but they can ask that faculties play a larger role in such determination.

Christians can also challenge the disciplinary organization of knowledge that determines the most academic part of the university's life. Do we truly learn about the real world when we attend to delimited aspects of that world as they lend themselves to study by specified methods? I believe the answer is negative. The concentration on method obscures those aspects of the world that do not lend themselves to the approved methods, often quantitative ones. Further, the separation of distinguishable aspects of the world from their interconnection with one another omits all those features of reality that depend on these interconnections. In short, the ever-growing body of information produced by the academic disciplines is highly abstracted from the world about which it purports to inform us.

To say that abstraction occurs in academic disciplines is not to fault them. Abstraction characterizes all thinking. But good thinking is aware of its abstractions and tries to check itself against the concrete. Unfortunately, in the most prestigious academic disciplines, the abstractness is rarely noted, and few cautions are directed toward those who forget that abstraction has occurred. Conclusions are repeatedly drawn about the actual world from theories whose basis is an abstraction from the world.

It is not enough to point out questionable features of present universities. To judge them sensibly one must consider other options. I suggest that the university adopt wisdom as its primary goal rather than information. Of course, information is needed, but it should not be sought for its own sake. What information is to be sought should be determined by wisdom rather than by the methods in vogue at any given time in the advance of particular disciplines. Specialization should be around topics that need to be studied for the sake of attaining wisdom and implementing the ends dictated by wisdom.

A simple exercise will suggest how different the result would be. Consider some of the most pressing problems facing our society and the planet. Most lists would include some of the following: the pressure on the biosphere of population growth compounded by increasing per capita consumption on the part of the affluent; massive hunger around the world compounded by the use of land for export crops rather than food for local people and by the deterioration of agricultural land; the widespread alienation in our cities; the growing gap between rich and poor globally and within our own country; a spiritual vacuum often filled by irresponsible beliefs; our inability to solve international problems without resorting to violence; and the widespread tendency to depreciate and exploit women and ethnic minorities.

I do not want to insist on my list. Other Christians will identify other problems. After one has done so, one can ask where to turn in the university for guidance in dealing with one or more of the problems identified. Which department encourages its scholars to give attention to this question? Probably one will be hard-pressed to find any. Of course, there are departments that produce information useful in discerning and implementing wise policies, but that is a different matter. The same information can also be used in mindless ways.

There are wise people teaching in universities. Fortunately, they are not altogether excluded. Occasionally a philosophy department, for example, will hire an original thinker rather than someone to cover a particular field of study. Applied philosophy is becoming accepted in many departments as a legitimate field of study. And here and there are departments that identify their goals as relevance to some of the world's needs. But in general one will not look to philosophy departments for wisdom about how to deal with our most urgent problems. Similarly, there may be wise teachers in departments of physics or of English, but there is nothing about these departments that encourages such wisdom. Wisdom is found in the university despite, not because of, the basic assumptions that order its life.

If the university did accept wisdom as its goal rather than the production of specialized information, it would continue to encourage specialization within its faculty. But such specialization would be around the problem of overcoming hunger and alienation, or avoiding violence and ecological destruction, or responding to the spiritual crisis of the postmodern world, or attaining justice for Blacks or women. The list of needs is very long. A university organized to help human beings learn how to respond to such needs would be a very different institution from any we now have.

My purpose in making these proposals is not to predetermine what Christians would advocate for institutions of higher education if we decided to engage in theological reflection about them. It is, instead, to indicate that very important issues are at stake and that there are alternatives to the form that such institutions now take. It is also to show that Christian beliefs and values can be brought to bear in thinking about such matters in ways that can broaden the discussion for those who are not Christian. Christians are not the only people who favor the primacy of wisdom over information.

Critique of the Academic Discipline of Theology

The second section above considered what it would mean to engage in practical Christian thinking about some of the major institutions of our society. Any of these critical discussions could be continued in much more detail. When this is done, practical Christian thinking takes on life and relevance.

The persons who can best engage in such criticism are those who are immediately involved in the institutions. Professional clergy certainly have a role to play in the critique of the church, although even here it would be desirable for laypeople to play the primary role. But with respect to the other institutions, it is those lay Christians whose work falls within them who are best able to criticize. The critique of institutions should develop naturally out of reflection on lay Christian vocations.

As one whose professional life has fallen within higher education, I selected the university for particular criticism. But that criticism made clear that it can be only a beginning. Most of the university is organized into departments responsible for academic disciplines. These disciplines require more detailed criticism.

My own academic discipline has been theology. In many ways this whole book is a critique of academic theology. This theology has accepted its role within the university as one discipline alongside others. Its subject matter has been taken to be the Bible and the Christian tradition. Its task is to interpret that tradition. Its methods are primarily hermeneutical, and much of its energy is expended on refinement and application of hermeneutical methods.

In this process, it has lost touch with the real life of laypeople in the churches. Of course, tangentially, there are connections. Laypeople are interested in the Bible, and Bible scholars can answer some of their questions. But, in general, biblical scholars work for the advancement of their academic disciplines rather than to answer questions that arise out of church life. The same is true of church historians and systematic theologians. It is somewhat less true of Christian ethicists, but even they frame their research as often in terms of where their methods can be applied as in terms of the urgent needs of the church and individual Christians for guidance on ethical questions.

This book proposes other ways of thinking about theology growing out of general Christian experience and need. Professional theologians can assist in many ways. Their disciplinary work is relevant. Perhaps some will join in the tasks outlined here. But basically theology is a responsibility of all Christians, and that means primarily of lay Christians.

One strength of academic theology is that it studies its own history critically. It associates theological beliefs with fundamental assumptions and so engages in pressing received theologies for their deepest presuppositions. It is probably the most self-critical of academic disciplines. This self-criticism has reached new heights recently.

In the past two decades we have become aware in the church and in academic theology of how androcentric we have been. That is, we see that we have taken the male perspective as normative and virtually ignored the experience and sensibilities of women. We are becoming aware also of how profound the changes will be that we can anticipate in all our thinking when the perspective of women is recognized as of equal, and sometimes superior, validity for Christians.

We have also become aware of how Eurocentric we have been. We have read all history from the point of view of how it affected, or was affected by, what happened in Europe, and especially modern Western Europe. We have judged other cultures by their approximation to, or their difference from, the European, assuming that the European is normative and superior. We are only beginning to appreciate other ways of viewing what has happened on this planet, ways that relativize the European perspective and also show that in many respects it is peculiarly responsible for massive forms of evil.

Furthermore, we have come to see that we have viewed all reality from an anthropocentric point of view. That is, we have taken human beings to be the only truly important parts of the creation and seen all other creatures as instruments to our ends. In spite of our claims to be theocentric, we have in fact viewed God as belonging to us humans alone and as separate from the remainder of creation. As a result we have tolerated and even encouraged the ruthless exploitation and abuse of other creatures for short-run gains to human beings, often, indeed, to some human beings at the expense of most others.

These criticisms are first and foremost directed at ourselves as Christians. That is as it should be. Unless we criticize ourselves with particular rigor and care, we are in no position to criticize others. But after we have repented, that is, turned in new directions ourselves, after we have honed our critical skills on our own tradition and present institutions and our own theology, then it is legitimate to criticize others as well.

Indeed, such criticism is not only acceptable, it is badly needed. Christians cannot but care what happens in human society and to the planet as a whole. This is God's world and these are people whom God loves. The way our political and economic leaders think is of immense importance in what happens in this world and to these people. How they think, in turn, is deeply affected by the way they have been educated in their universities and the advice they receive from those who are shaped by other academic disciplines. For these reasons, Christians cannot be indifferent to the assumptions that underlie disciplines other than theology.

Critique of the Academic Discipline of Economics

All of these disciplines have their importance, and according to the interest and expertise of lay Christians, they may be called to examine any of them. But the discipline that most profoundly affects public policy in our world is economics. Today the primary goal of most governments and international agencies is economic improvement. Accordingly, economists are those most frequently called on for advice and guidance. Hence, it is particularly important to ask whether this advice and guidance directs energies in appropriate directions.

This question is to be answered first by examining what happens in actual history when governments follow the direction recommended by those most fully shaped by academic economics. In general, production of goods and services increases, but there are social and environmental costs. For those who are primarily interested in increasing consumption, the former point is very important and the latter minor; but for most Christians, the latter point is also important. Our question is why the policies recommended by those best versed in the discipline of economics often have negative social and ecological consequences and why economists pay so little attention to these consequences. Hence, to illustrate a critique of the assumptions of an academic discipline other than theology, I select economics.

A cursory examination of economic theory quickly explains why policies recommended by economists produce economic growth. The most important assumption of economic theory is that the goal of economic policies is to foster growth. Indeed, economic theory is primarily the theory of how to make the economy grow.

Since great genius has been invested in the development of this theory, it is not surprising that its application in the real world often succeeds in generating economic growth.

Our inquiry is also as to why recommended economic policies so often have negative social and ecological effects and why so few economists give major attention to these. The answer with respect to the social dimension is that the human beings whose well-being economics is designed to foster are not understood to be social or communal in nature. They are viewed as separable and autonomous individuals whose interests lie in consuming as much as possible in exchange for working as little as possible. This good is furthered by increased production per unit of time devoted to labor. This, in turn, is furthered by specialization in larger and larger markets, which leads to breaking up traditional communities. In the terms of the recent self-criticism of Christian theology, this view of human beings can be understood as androcentric and Eurocentric in the extreme.

The destruction of nature accompanying so many policies recommended by economists reflects the thoroughgoing anthropocentrism of economic theory. Nature appears in this theory only peripherally under the heading of land. Land was once thought of as one of the factors of production, but is now considered chiefly in terms of resources.

These resources are treated as, for all practical purposes, unlimited, so that the only important question for economics is the cost of procuring them and turning them into humanly desired products. The goal is to do so with as little expenditure of labor as possible, so that human beings can gain more goods for less work. We see the results in the mining of the soil, unsustainable use of renewable resources, the rapid exhaustion of nonrenewable ones, and the many forms of pollution.

These assumptions are so deeply entrenched in mainstream economic theory that many economists regard them as defining economics. To seek goals other than increased production with other assumptions about humanity and nature would not be, for them, economics. Sometimes, dismissively, they call reflection about such alternatives "theology." Accordingly, it is appropriate for us as theologians to show that a different formulation of the good, based on different assumptions, could provide a basis for normative reflection about the economy. I suggest as an alternative goal of economics the well-being of persons-in-community, that is, of human beings understood as fundamentally social in character.

To avoid arguing about such different identifications of ends, economists may assert that by growth, that is, by increasing production, the economy is making what contribution it can to the well-being of human communities. They have no tools for measuring the well-being of human communities in general, but they do have tools for measuring production. Hence, they stay with their goal.

We now have a factual question by which the validity of the dominant assumption of the academic discipline of economics can be tested. Do the policies encouraged by economists so as to increase production actually make the greatest contribution the economy can make to the well-being of the community? If so, then calling attention to the assumption that growth is the proper end of economic policy would be a largely idle, merely pedantic, exercise.

However, it is overwhelmingly evident that the policies that have been adopted for the sake of growth have not always contributed to the well-being of communities. Take the period since World War II in the United States and consider one industrial suburb in the Midwest, one rural village in Kansas, and one city in the Northeast. The chances are that the industrial suburb has lost its economic base and its character as a community, the Kansas village has disappeared, and the Eastern city is suffering from urban blight.

But perhaps I have won too easy a victory. Perhaps decay of community in the United States is the result of forces that are not economic. No doubt there are other forces at work. But it is clear that the application of economic principles to society inherently and inevitably works against stable community.

This is quite explicit in economic teaching. In order for the economy to grow, capital must be used as efficiently as possible. That means, of course, that it is also used as profitably as possible; so those who possess capital have every incentive to cooperate in the needed policies. For capital to be used as efficiently as possible it should flow freely to those places where it can be most profitably invested. This means that the owner of capital should not continue the operation of a factory, even if it is profitable, if the closing of the factory would make possible a more profitable investment elsewhere. We have seen the result in factory closings in the Midwest and throughout the country. The ideal of the economist is that labor follow capital, and of course much of it does, since capital means jobs. Undercutting the economies of hundreds of industrial suburbs is a direct working out of economic theory and the policies it dictates.

What about the destruction of the town in Kansas? That, too, is a direct outgrowth of the application of economic principles, this time to agriculture. Here, however, the emphasis should be placed on labor productivity rather than capital profitability, although the two are closely linked.

Economists point out that total product is a function of the number of hours of work and of the amount of production per hour. If the number of hours of work is held constant, then the total production can increase only as the productivity of labor rises. This productivity rises as capital, chiefly in the form of fossil fuels and machines, is applied to the production. If there is no need for increased product in the sector in which productivity is rising, then labor can shift from that sector to others.

In abstract terms this describes the very concrete changes that have occurred in rural America. The application of capital to agriculture greatly reduced the need for labor. Hence, most of the people who formerly worked on their own farms, or for others, have now gone to the cities. Of course, capital can be applied to agriculture best when the farms are very large; so policy has been geared to promote large-scale farming. This has been very successful. It has, of course, meant that the villages that once dotted rural America have no economic base in the service of a rural population.

Can we blame urban blight also on policies that are geared to economic principles? Not directly. It has multiple causes. But two of them are surely capital flight and the fact that not all of those displaced from agriculture have been able to enter into the mainstream of the urban economy. As long as there are workers available elsewhere who are better prepared to fit the demands of industry, capital would be foolish to locate in the areas to which the displaced rural population has migrated. Economic policies geared to growth have contributed to the problem.

Economic principles weaken communities such as cities in another way. They call for the continuing enlargement of markets. Markets are enlarged as goods and capital flow freely over larger and larger areas. This means an increasing concentration of economic power at greater distance from most of the places where production is carried out.

Thus, forty years ago much of the ownership of the productive capacities located in a city was likely to be in the hands of persons who lived there. They had an interest in the well-being of the community. They had a natural preference for making their investments succeed in that city rather than moving them elsewhere. But today, this is no longer true. Control of the large-scale productive and commercial enterprises located in the city is likely to be in the hands of people who do not live there. The managers who do live in the city move frequently. Little civic spirit develops in the business community, if the word *community* has any meaning here. Further, if the city, for the sake of community goals in the area of environment, health, or safety, places restrictions on business that reduce its profit, business has little incentive to remain. If the city wants to keep the jobs, it must allow the distant managers of capital to set the terms.

It is safe, therefore, to say that the application of economic principles geared to growth has had a drastic negative effect on existing communities. If the economists were really willing to stake their claim on the argument that economic growth contributes to the well-being of existing communities, they would be easily defeated. But that has never been their real meaning. Their claim is that the new communities that come into being as a result of their policies are more prosperous, hence better off, than were the ones that economic growth has destroyed. The evidence for this is that their per capita income is higher.

Is it true that the new communities are better as communities than the ones they have displaced? It *is* true that many of them are more affluent. However, by other measures the average community in this country is inferior to its predecessors. Among these measures are family stability, crime, drug abuse, and participation in political processes. Also, despite real per-pupil increases in expenditure on schooling, there is near unanimity that the quality of public education has declined.

But can these declines be attributed in any important way to the economy? Yes. The growth-oriented economy makes for more rapid movements of population. Fewer people participate or feel responsibility for community institutions. The decline of community feeling is connected with the rise of crime and drug abuse. Mobile families without community support are less stable. The connection is vividly illustrated in education. Studies have shown that the achievement of students correlates most closely with parental interest in the school. Clearly there is less such interest than before. It is hard to doubt that the more stable communities displaced by today's more fluid ones fostered more parental involvement in community schools.

Despite the intuitive plausibility of these judgments, they cannot be proved. Further, losses in some areas cannot be statistically compared with gains in per capita income. Hence, economists cannot be refuted to their own satisfaction in their claim that the goal of the economy is to contribute as many desired goods and services as possible for the consumption of the people.

The fact that so many economists cling to this view despite its lack of plausibility suggests socialization into a way of thinking more than an open appraisal of the evidence. Their whole system of thought, with its powerful analytic and prescriptive tools, is built on this assumption. Nothing internal to the discipline encourages its reexamination. In the innumerable detailed discussions on which economists concentrate their attention, they find enough vindication of expectations to confirm the value of the system.

Commitment to growth is shared by market and centrally planned economies. The argument between them has been partly over issues of justice and personal liberty, but it has also been over which could more successfully attain the growth that both desired. The collapse of the centrally planned economies of Eastern Europe has settled the latter argument. This has led to considerable complacency on the part of economists committed to growth through the free market. They are less interested than ever in reconsidering their basic assumptions.

Because we viewed the commitment of economic policy to the overall increase of production as disastrous, a group of us conducted a study that limits itself to the economists' world of things that can be measured in dollars. We suspected that even when the measure of well-being is limited in this way, increased production is often a poor way of promoting it. We believe we have shown that this is the case.

No economist claims that all production contributes to economic well-being, and most economists acknowledge that improvement of economic well-being is the appropriate goal of economic policies. They justify their neglect of the difference between per capita Gross National Product and national economic well-being by arguing, or assuming, that on the whole the advance of the former improves the latter as well. This has been questioned from time to time, and statistics have been offered in support and in opposition to the theory. It is into this discussion that we entered by developing an Index of Sustainable Economic Welfare (ISEW).

We began our calculations, like all who have attempted to measure economic well-being, with personal consumption, thus accepting the questionable assumption of economists that, on the whole, the increase of consumption contributes to the economic well-being of the consumer. However, we then adjusted this total figure by considering distribution. Our assumption is that the community as a whole is improved more when increased consumption goes to its poorest members rather than to those who already have enough.

We also considered community through time. A nation is economically better off when its present consumption is not at the expense of its future citizens, that is, when its consumption is sustainable. Using up its capital assets and natural resources without replacing them is unsustainable.

Our results, like those of most others who have attempted this kind of study, show that improvement in economic well-being has been much slower than that in per capita GNP in recent decades. Indeed, according to our figures, sustainable economic well-being declined in the eighties, while the per capita GNP continued to climb.

Although critics are correct when they point out that every attempt to measure economic well-being is fraught with disputable elements, so that nothing can ever be "proved" in this way, nevertheless, we and others have shown that the rise of GNP can be accompanied by declining well-being, even when we ignore such social indicators as crime and drug abuse.

In response to these strong indications that economic growth no longer benefits people economically, few economists are trying to offer counterevidence. The continuing assumption of most of them that the difference between quantity of production and economic well-being can be ignored attests to the depth of their immersion in their theories and their lack of any sense of need to justify their assumptions. The hope must be that well-meaning citizens and policymakers can recognize the difference ignored by the academic discipline of economics and cease to assume that increased production is the magical solution to all problems.

The alternative suggested by the ISEW did not challenge the anthropocentrism of standard economics. It simply shifts from the goal of increasing production to that of improving the well-being of persons-in-community. A more adequate statement of the good that economics should serve would be the well-being of the earth as a whole. This would lead to a more radical critique of current economic theory and practice.

Conclusions

Christian reflection about vocations should be vigorously renewed. It is important both in itself and as an entry into other forms of theological activity for which laypeople are well-qualified. This chapter has emphasized especially the importance of laypeople analyzing the assumptions of the institutions in which they work, proposing better ones, and projecting the changes that would follow from new assumptions. Most laypeople can participate in this form of theology.

The chapter proceeded to a discussion of the academic disciplines. This is not accessible to all laypeople. It is a natural step primarily for those in higher education. But those in other traditional professions are also closely related to some of the academic disciplines. And all Christians have reason to be interested in the results of the critique of disciplines, since so many policies affecting them are influenced by the assumptions of the disciplines.

The critique of academic disciplines, therefore, is not itself a merely "academic" exercise. The critique of academic theology is for the sake of the the church and of the world as well. Unless the meaning of "theology" is separated from its narrowing to academic theology and authoritarian pronouncements, the church is destined to continue to decay, and the contribution the world so badly needs from Christians will not be made.

The critique of academic economics is for the sake of supporting public policies different from those encouraged by most economists. An example will illustrate how important these differences can be. Currently the United States is confronted with basic decisions about trade policy. Its administration has led in the Uruguay Round of the General Agreement on Tariffs and Trade (GATT), and it has negotiated with Canada and Mexico the North American Free Trade Agreement (NAFTA). Both of these advance the cause of free trade and as such implement the ideals stemming from the academic discipline of economics. As long as Christians continue to turn to economic experts for guidance on economic questions, we will support agreements of this sort.

But suppose we decide that the economic well-being of human beings as persons-in-community is more important than quantity of production. In that case we will ask different questions about the effects of these treaties. Granted they will lead to increasing production as the economists assure us, how will they affect human communities now and in the future? Is the continuing downward pressure on wages and workplace conditions in our country good for its people as a whole? Can the natural environment sustain the pressure of increased production? Is the quality of life improved as established communities are destroyed and mobility further increased?

Since my own answers to all these questions are negative, I am opposed to the proposed GATT and the NAFTA. But this is not the place to argue particular policy questions. It *is* the place to illustrate how important consequences follow from the usually unexamined assumptions of academic disciplines. It *is* the place to invite lay Christians to critique the assumptions of those disciplines—and professions and institutions—they know best.

Theology
as
Transforming
Tradition

The Tradition of Church Theology

Chapter 2 dealt with one very important form of theology, one that I call practical Christian thinking. This is the form of theology that forces itself most insistently on individual Christians as they try to live their lives and on the church as it seeks to be faithful in its work and witness. Chapter 3 extended this practical concern to critical reflection on work, on the institutions that shape our society, and on the academic disciplines.

As one presses practical Christian thinking further and further it can become the basis for every other form of theology. But that would be a long and indirect approach to some of the tasks to which attention should be directed. One very important matter about which we should think intentionally as Christians is our Christian heritage. Too often this task

is left to professional academic specialists. The renewal of
the church will not occur until laypeople join in reflection of
this kind.

We live out of a history of which we are only partly aware
but which exerts enormous influence upon us. Much of that
influence is profoundly positive, but we cannot assume that
this is always the case. Indeed, the liberation theologians,
whom we considered in the first chapter, have pointed out
that the weight of tradition is often oppressive rather than
redemptive. We grow as Christian thinkers when we take this
seriously and reflect about how we are now to relate to what
has been believed in the community that has shaped us.

I have postponed dealing with this topic because it seems
less closely related to the lives of most lay Christians. Reflection on practice is more obviously relevant. Yet if that reflection truly *is* intentionally Christian, it cannot escape the question of what responsible Christian belief is today. Even if, on
this question, laypeople need more help from professionals,
that does not make it less important. Nor does it reduce their
responsibility to make up their own minds. Professionals can
provide historical information and suggestions about how
best to think about the past. No Christian can tell another
what finally to conclude. Only a community in which each
person takes responsibility for her or his belief can be a
healthy Christian community.

Chapter 1 devoted a good deal of space to explaining
what I mean by theology: intentional Christian thinking
about important matters. The definition of theology is one
very important matter for us to think about as Christians,
that is, it is a theological task. If I had simply defined theology and then plunged in, the reader might not have noticed
how many assumptions and judgments I was making in that
process. If I am to encourage lay theology, I need to make
my definition and my reasons for it as explicit as possible. It
is because of the way that I define theology that I consider it
an essential activity for lay Christians. It is that definition

that led naturally to chapters on practical Christian think-ing, since so many of the important matters on which Chris-tians reflect are indeed directly practical.

Now the question is how theology proceeds when its important questions have to do with our Christian heritage or tradition. Here further specifications or definitions are required. My own judgments and values enter into these specifications more controversially than into the general call for practical Christian thinking. To enable the reader to be critical of my choices, I will make them as explicit as pos-sible.

The title of this chapter is "Theology as Transforming Tradition." That title already assumes a lot. It assumes, for example, that tradition is not satisfactory as it stands. The first chapter pointed out that Christian treatment of Jews has been deeply affected by inherited beliefs. There is now wide agreement that the way these inherited beliefs shape us is not satisfactory. The discussion of liberation theologies agreed with them that Christianity has often functioned oppressively. Comments about the ecological crisis implied that traditional formulations of theology have often blinded us to what we have been doing to the natural environment.

Those who *are* generally satisfied with inherited beliefs might entitle this chapter "Transmitting and Applying Tra-dition." Those who are largely satisfied, but still recognize that some modification of tradition is needed, might write about "Adapting Tradition." Others, who see more need for change, could take as a topic "Reforming Tradition." My choice of "transforming" assumes that the changes needed are greater than those titles suggest.

Another assumption is expressed by the choice of the term *tradition* rather than *Bible* as the focus. Protestants some-times contrast the Bible as the word of God with tradition as the words of human beings. One who holds that position might prefer as a title, "Theology as Interpretation of the Bible" or, if one felt the need for change, "Theology as Reinterpretation of the Bible." To define theology in relation to tradition instead of the Bible assumes that the contrast between the Bible and the subsequent tradition is not so sharp. However profoundly inspired by God, the Bible is also a very human book. And however human the subsequent tradition has been, Christians still find God at work in it. Indeed, the Bible is part of the tradition, the most authoritative part according to the remainder of the tradition.

My choice of title for this chapter assumes both that the received tradition is in need of drastic change and that the Bible is included in the tradition as its most authoritative part. It also assumes that the inherited tradition is, for most of us, the place to start. That is, however fully we acknowledge the problems with inherited Christianity, we do not look elsewhere for a preferable starting point. In this respect, the point of view expressed in this title is profoundly conservative. The starting point I am proposing is not the experience of the oppressed or the most adequate worldview, although I consider both to be legitimate starting points for some. Nor is it a neutral philosophical or scientific perspective, although valuable work can be done in that way also.

I propose that we start with the Christian heritage, recognizing that this is what has shaped us and what motivates us now to change. The immediate stimulus for change often comes from external critique, but the openness to hearing that critique, the willingness to recognize the elements of truth it contains, and the commitment to repent and reform ourselves in light of that critical truth—all this comes from our faith as awakened in us through the tradition.

If the task before us is to transform Christian tradition, the next question is: *which* Christian tradition? There are many. First, there are the distinct traditions of the Eastern and Western churches and, within the West, of Roman Catholics and Protestants. Among Protestants there are the Lutheran, Calvinist, Anglican, and left-wing traditions. And this still greatly simplifies a vast complexity.

I stand in the Wesleyan tradition, so inevitably my thinking about tradition in general is colored by that. Yet I am impressed by the remarkable achievements of the ecumenical movement. Through its Faith and Order program it has not only clarified the real differences among the traditions, it has also shown how much they can come to have in common as they recover shared roots, interact with one another, and learn from one another. The ancient divisions have been overcome almost to the point that it has become meaningful to speak of *the* Christian tradition.

Yet, in the meantime, other branches of Christianity, which have not participated in these discussions or been deeply affected by them, have become more important on the world scene. Just as it seemed that ecumenical Christianity was moving toward theological unity, competing expressions of the Christian faith have become prominent. Even so, I shall speak of "church theology," meaning by that both the particular teachings of particular churches and the affirmations of the conciliar movement.

In this chapter, then, we are considering the transformation of the tradition of church theology. This transformation should be in light of all that the church can learn from the tradition of academic theology whose separation from church theology was discussed in Chapter 1. The transformation should also be the light that all Christians can learn from the many valid criticisms directed against us from the outside, which have become inescapable during the past quarter century.

I approach all these matters in that subtradition of both academic theology and church theology that is called "process theology." I understand process theology as a proposal for the transformation of church theology along the lines indicated. Prior to the sixties it was primarily a proposal for the transformation of church theology in terms of certain developments in academic theology. The explosion of criticism of both church and academic theology in the sixties took church theologians by surprise. Process theologians were as surprised by the new developments as any others. Nevertheless, process theology, more than most other forms of church theology, was able to absorb and affirm the new critical insights, thereby being itself transformed. Its self-understanding required this acceptance of its own transformation.

Creative Transformation

The most basic contribution process theology can make is its support and clarification of the process of transformation itself. Process theologians have no monopoly on the call for transformation. Indeed, it is part of the understanding of process theology that this call is inherent in the Christian message. Others have made proposals for specific forms of transformation more effectively than have process theologians. But for no other community of discourse has this term been so central or the process to which it points so analytically, or so theologically, considered.

Actually the full term, as introduced into the discussion by Henry Nelson Wieman, is "creative transformation." The modifier makes clear that what it names is not simply any change of form, but a positive one. However, this positive element is generally heard in the word *transformation* even when it stands alone. In this book "transformation" is always shorthand for "creative transformation."

Why is the idea of transformation so important today? I will state my answer existentially, believing that what is true for me personally is true for many other Christians as well. If to be a Christian today meant accepting any past or present form of Christianity as normative, I could not be a Christian. For example, virtually all of Christianity to this date has been both anti-Jewish and patriarchal. These have not been superficial accretions easily set aside; they have been pervasive features of its life and thought deriving from and affecting its core doctrinal formulations as well as much of its practice. The exceptions to these generalizations that historical accuracy allows and requires are important sources of hope, but they do not provide a full-blown model that can now be reenacted. To continue to think and act now as Christians have thus far thought and acted is to be anti-Jewish and patriarchal. If being a Christian is being anti-Jewish and patriarchal, I cannot in good conscience remain a Christian.

But if Christianity is anti-Jewish and patriarchal to its core, and if I reject this, then am I not rejecting Christianity? The answer is "Yes" if Christianity is defined by any of the forms it has embodied thus far. But I do not understand Christianity in this way. I understand it as a movement that is most true to itself when it changes in appropriate ways as it gains new understanding and faces new challenges. I experience my own revulsion against anti-Judaism and patriarchalism as itself arising out of that history and its deepest commitments. It is anti-Judaism and patriarchalism that seem unChristian to me, not my rejection of them. Thus my rejection of the normativeness of all past forms of Christianity is an expression of my Christian faith.

According to my understanding of Christian faith, a major vocation of the Christian is to transform Christianity. My Christian commitment is to this transformation. We will not transform Christianity once and for all and then have the transformed Christianity to which we can commit ourselves. Our best achievements will themselves need transformation. It is in the transforming that I find the effective presence of the living God. My deepest commitment is to this process of creative transformation rather than to any one of its products. That is one reason why I call myself a "process theologian."

We do not transform Christianity by simply announcing our repudiation of objectionable features in its past. If we deleted from our heritage everything that is in any way objectionable, we would have nothing left. Those who move in this direction step by step, not realizing that they are peeling an onion, have given to a once vital "liberalism" a bad name. The transformed Christianity for which we are working will be at least as theologically rich, confident in its affirmations, and demanding in its implications as any past form. Transformation is not away from wholehearted, all-inclusive commitment, but toward forms of such commitment that will direct Christian energies into paths that will heal the world God loves rather than destroy it.

Faith in Christ

This discussion of transforming the tradition has been somewhat formal and abstract. It is time to take up examples. The problem of Christian anti-Judaism has been highlighted, and it will serve to suggest an area of creative transformation of church teaching that is in process today.

This problem is multifaceted. There is the negative image of the Pharisees in the Synoptic Gospels. There is the unrelieved hostility to "the Jews" in John. There is the supersessionist contrasting of the new covenant with the old. There is the blaming of the crucifixion on the Jews rather than the Romans, with Judas in particular standing for Jews in the Christian imagination. All of this requires fresh theological reflection and transformation of the tradition.

Central to Christian anti-Judaism as well as to its pejorative attitude toward other religious communities is another doctrine more obviously central to its life. That is its Christology. Christians have believed that, in the words of Acts 4:12b, "there is no other name under heaven given among mortals by which we must be saved" than the name of Jesus Christ. Indeed, that salvation is only through Christ has often been taken to be the very heart of the Christian gospel. If human beings can be saved only through explicit faith in Jesus, and if Jews refuse to believe in him, then Christians must teach that Jews are not saved, that their saving relation to God ended when the new covenant arose. And, of course, the same is true of Muslims, Hindus, Buddhists, and participants in primal religions.

But today we encounter Jews, Muslims, Hindus, Buddhists, and members of primal religions whose personal spiritual depth and authenticity we cannot question. Many of them have great wisdom, including insights that we have not gained from our own tradition. Must we assert that they are, nevertheless, denied salvation and hence do everything we can to convert them? Faithfulness to our heritage seems to call on us to do this, and many Christians repeatedly renew their commitment to this enterprise. If we refuse to do so, we seem to be eroding that heritage, simply dropping off those parts of it that do not fit our present sensibility. If our goal is transformation rather than elimination, how shall we proceed?

We need to begin by going more deeply into our faith in Christ. How does it function for us? How is it functioning at the moment we are considering our proper response to the spiritual authenticity of those who do not share our faith? Is it functioning to make us prejudge that whatever they say is false or, at least, beside the point? Or is it functioning to lead us to listen to them and to learn from them? Perhaps the answer is that it functions in part in both ways. Then we will ask: which is the most authentic? Does Christ call us to prejudge negatively what these people have to say? Does Christ call us to try to force them to believe something that does not seem to them true? Or does Christ call us to listen and learn?

As I reflect about this, I find that I understand Christ as continually challenging the values and sense of reality that I have established and within which I find security. This includes any structure of beliefs I have come to affirm, including beliefs about Christ. Christ calls me to take the other as seriously as myself, and that means also to take the other's way of thinking and feeling as seriously as my own. That does not mean that I accept everything that others tell me. But it does mean that when I discern spiritual authenticity in another, I acknowledge it and take seriously what the other tells me. It means that if the other tells me things that are new to me, yet ring true, I will not reject them because the source is one who does not profess to be a Christian. Faithfulness to Christ calls me to listen and learn, even if what I hear is disconcerting and painful.

What more does faithfulness to Christ require? I cannot be satisfied simply to gain new information and ideas and add these to what I now hold. If they are disconcerting and painful, they must be in tension with other ideas I have long cherished. What am I to do?

Consider an example that will keep attention on Christology. Perhaps I have been talking with a Jew who points out that Christian evangelization of Jews threatens the integrity of the peoplehood of Israel. She has said that the Christian strategy of opening a primarily Christian society to Jewish participation and then seeking to convert individual Jews to Christian churches is a greater threat to the survival of the Jewish people than were the pogroms of Europe.

How can I incorporate what I have learned into my faith in Christ? Must I say that whatever Jews think they want, faithfulness to Christ requires that I share the good news with them and welcome individual Jews into the fellowship of Christian faith? Or must I say that Christ is good news for me but damaging to Jews? Must I surrender my assumptions about Christ's universal relevance?

There are several ways Christians have responded to these issues that are creatively transforming Christology. My personal emphasis is that Christians have sinned against Jews too massively and too continuously to be in position to present Christ to them. Furthermore, Jesus was a Jew, and there is no reason to cease to be a Jew in order to appropriate the insights of Jesus. That does not mean for me that Jews do not need Jesus. It does mean that we can believe that once Jews are sufficiently free from Christian pressure, they can carry through their own study of Jesus as a Jewish teacher. They will then be able to incorporate what they learn into an enriched Judaism. To appropriate the meaning of Jesus for them may never involve associating with him the name "Christ," so precious to us. But they will be able to teach us much about faithfulness to Jesus that we have missed in our anti-Jewish Gentile traditions. Indeed, some of this is already happening.

This creative transformation of my understanding of Jesus Christ is, I feel sure, an expression of faithfulness to Christ. It is rooted in Paul's letter to the Romans, chapters 9—11, but it need not claim to represent Paul's exact intention. My withdrawal from evangelization of Jews is not a compromise or erosion of my faith. It is a deepening of faith through a transformation of understanding. Having learned what I have learned, to persist in efforts at persuading individual Jews to join Christian churches would be unfaithful.

If Christ is the source of my openness to the other and of my creative transformation through the other, do I think that Christ has universal meaning? Yes, my faithfulness to Christ leads me to believe that human beings in general need to become more open to one another and more willing to be transformed by what they learn from one another.

The question is whether Christ is the only source of openness and of creative transformation through what one learns from the other. If it were clear that this were so, then there would be strong grounds for evangelization of the world. But there are good reasons for hesitation. First, for many Christians, beliefs about Jesus Christ function as a reason for closure and fixity and sometimes of aggression against others. The task of converting *Christians* to the true meaning of Christ is very large. And because Christian closure has such disturbing results in today's world, this mission may have priority over the evangelization of others. Second, at least some of the others find reasons for openness and transformation in their own traditions without reference to Christ.

We Christians may discern the working of Christ in their midst, but they identify this working in other ways. To whatever extent they do so, then this function of Christ in itself may not suffice as reason to evangelize.

However, my own conclusion is not as opposed to evangelization as these comments may suggest. Although I do see principles of self-critical openness in other religious communities, I see them there because in faithfulness to Christ I look for them. But I do not find that openness to transformation is so fully built into any other scripture as into the Jewish and Christian ones, or is as fully embodied in our scripture anywhere else as in Jesus Christ. Indeed, I see the creatively transforming power of God as uniquely incarnate in Jesus. I believe there *is* a universal message universally needed, and we should share this even when our own house is not in order.

In our day, as we struggle to end the epoch of Christian arrogance and imperialism, it is important to reemphasize the uniqueness of Jesus Christ. Otherwise there is danger that sensitive Christians will simply delete central beliefs rather than transform them. But it is equally important to affirm that other traditions may also have principles of universal relevance and saving power to share. After so many centuries of talking without listening, Christ calls us to listen more and speak less.

Transformation and Purification

The creative transformation of tradition is not just a recent phenomenon developing in response to criticisms of Christianity. The history of Israel was a series of creative transformations. The Hebrews were profoundly influenced by Egyptians, Canaanites, Babylonians, Persians, and Greeks. But their internalization of the contributions of these people did not lead to fundamental discontinuity. The post-exilic Jews were very different from their forebears in the Davidic kingdom, and those were very different from the people who wandered in the desert. But the changes were attained by the transformation of the heritage, not by its abandonment. Also, this process of creative transformation of Judaism continued after the time that Christianity branched off from its Jewish stem.

A very profound change is attested in the New Testament. But this, too, was a creative transformation of the Jewish traditions out of which early Christianity grew. The Christians clung to the Jewish scriptures. They read them in new ways. But the church rejected the proposal that because these were Jewish they should be discarded and that Christianity should understand itself as a truly new religion.

As Christianity became primarily a Hellenistic movement, it was again transformed quite radically by the assimilation of Greek thought and spirituality. In the modern world, science, the Enlightenment, and the rise of historical consciousness have had impacts of comparable importance. The story goes on.

Of course, this picture greatly oversimplifies. "Creative transformation" ideally retains all the heritage that is rightly retained and integrates it with all the new stimulus that is rightly admitted. But in the real world, including the real church, what happens is never so perfect. In the actual processes of change, transformation is always mixed with failure to appreciate the true value of both the heritage and the external stimulus. Elements of both that should have been creatively synthesized are lost, and elements of both that should have been set aside are included.

The task is never finished, and there is a place for those who see their work more as purification than as creative transformation. Although in fact there were elements of creative transformation in the work of the Reformers and of the leaders of the twentieth-century Neo-Reformation movement, these Christians defined their goal more as renewal. This renewal involved purification and retrieval. In the process of renewal they purified the tradition of much from which it needed to be purified, but they also eliminated much that is required in the ongoing tradition. They exaggerated the separability of the Scriptures from the remainder of the historical process.

The dialectic of transformation and renewal is required for a healthy continuance of Christian tradition. That means that they are inseparably connected. There is an element of renewal in all creative transformation, and there can in fact be no renewal without some element of transformation. The accent must fall sometimes on one and sometimes on the other. The judgment as to when which is needed shapes the work of the theologian.

Today there is a deep divide among sensitive Christians on this issue. Viewing the decay in the church, there are some who believe that what is needed is renewal and the establishment of boundaries. Instead of openness to others, they believe, the priority should be given to deepening rootedness in our own heritage. In their view, the task is to socialize those who are now nominally Christian into a fuller appropriation of the symbols of the faith.

There are others, and I count myself among them, who believe that health cannot be found in that direction. The issues that have been raised in the past quarter century are authentic ones. We now know that our inherited symbol system demonizes Jews, dehumanizes women, and leads to insensitivity toward the earth. These problems will not go away just because we stop listening. We need a transformed symbol system that can evoke the deepest convictions and loyalties of the most sensitive and self-critical Christians.

In my view as a process theologian, renewal and transformation, despite their dialectical relation, are not on the same level. The larger goal is transformation. Elements of renewal should take place for the sake of transformation.

I am putting my cards on the table so that the reader can judge my case. I am thinking intentionally as a Christian about what is needed, and I want to encourage others to think intentionally as Christians about whether they agree or disagree. My purpose is to provide as much help as possible in making the decision.

Why do some take renewal as the goal whereas I affirm it as in the service of transformation? If one believes that the fullness of truth, or the adequate way of thinking and living, was present in some earlier version of the Christian tradition and is now obscured, then renewal is the proper response. The Reformers believed that all we need was given once and for all in the Bible. Hence the purification of the existing tradition of all that was in tension with the Bible and recovery of what had been lost was the natural and proper goal. Some Anglicans have seen the third century as providing a norm of this sort, and some Roman Catholics have looked to the thirteenth century. Some Calvinists look to Calvin's Geneva or to Knox's Scotland. On the formal point, the results are the same. If the church has fallen from an earlier purity, it needs renewal. That involves the removal of much that has been introduced into the later tradition and the retrieval of much that has been lost.

Much of positive importance has been achieved in these programs of renewal. Much that has been eliminated needed to be eliminated, and much that has been recovered needed to be recovered. But I celebrate these attainments more because these eliminations and recoveries made new appropriations possible than because what remains after the removals and retrievals suffices for all time. For example, the dethronement of Aristotelian philosophy by the Reformers and of Hegelian philosophy by the Neo-Reformation theologians opened the door to other philosophical insights. But when it is taken to mean that the questions posed by philosophy can be once and for all set aside, it is mistaken. Today much of positive importance can be achieved by renewing emphasis on the inherited symbol system in congregations and by teaching a new generation to think in traditional terms

and to act seriously *as Christians.* But part of acting seriously
as Christians is listening to others and learning from them.

My understanding is that the fullness of truth lies in the
future. I believe that in Jesus Christ we have a basis for evalu-
ating our inherited beliefs and for discerning what is true
and what is false in new ideas that we hear. Thus the fullness of truth is anticipated or foreshadowed in Jesus, but the
fullness of truth will include much that we can never learn
directly by reading our Bibles or studying our traditions.
Much of it we must learn from Socrates, from Gautama, from
Mohammed, from Maimonides, from Gandhi; also from
Hegel, Marx, Nietzsche, and Freud; and even from Thomas
Altizer, James Cone, Gustavo Gutierrez, and Rosemary
Ruether. The fullness of truth includes all their insights and
much more of which our generation has not yet begun to
dream. The Christian tradition in any of its past forms, in-
cluding the Bible, does not.

Today some who call for renewal do not insist on the
universal truth or relevance of the renewed Christianity at
which they aim. It is enough for them that it is one cultural-
linguistic system among others, as long as we affirm that it
is *ours.* As one who calls for transformation, I am not satisfied. Christianity in its present form, or in any of its past
forms, is, indeed, not universal. It omits much of redemptive value that other communities have found, and it lacks
much that is yet to be revealed in the future. But it serves a
Christ who has universal salvific meaning and relevance pre-
cisely because the service for which Christ calls is openness
to all truth and creative transformation through it. From this
point of view, to defend any particular form of Christianity
as final, even for a limited community, is to substitute an
idol for Christ and to block the working of the Holy Spirit.
But equally, to deny the universal meaning of Christ is to
betray much of what is true in our heritage.

There is another contrast that is even more important than
that between transformation and renewal. That is the differ-

ence between the process of watering down the faith, on the one side, and its creative transformation, on the other. If the word *liberal* has been so degraded as now to mean the former, then liberalism is responsible for the lukewarmness so prevalent in the oldline denominations. We must all oppose such degenerate "liberalism." But in the early part of this century, in the great days of the social gospel, that was *not* what liberalism meant. It was much more a commitment to renewing the fullness of a faith that had been truncated by an individualistic reading. It embodied a spirit of openness to learning from all those who could teach. If that is what is meant by liberalism, an enriched Christocentric liberalism is our hope.

Not all of the many voices to which we should listen today are in agreement. Hence even those who are willing to listen and learn find difficulties in doing so. Furthermore, the process of transformation of the tradition is not subject merely to goodwill. It requires creative imagination and mutual support, extensive experimentation, and willingness to try again after failures. The theological task is demanding, but not obscure or irrelevant.

The Doctrine of God

The remainder of this chapter offers additional examples of the creative transformation of the tradition. These deal with God and God's way of relating to the world. They are topics that impinge directly on ordinary Christian piety. They are also close to the hearts of process theologians.

Process theologians do not work alone on the creative transformation of the doctrine of God. Others share our goals, and they have often been more effective than we. The reader may agree with the specific transformations of the doctrine of God that are proposed without accepting the process standpoint. But the reader can also better evaluate what is said when I make fully explicit the perspective from which I write.

In the tradition there have been two doctrines about God that both of my philosophical mentors, Alfred North Whitehead and Charles Hartshorne, opposed with particular vigor. Since neither philosopher identified himself as a Christian theologian, it would be hard to say that they opposed these doctrines primarily as Christians. Yet Whitehead juxtaposed what he saw as objectionable in the traditional Christian doctrine to the message of Jesus. And Hartshorne developed his doctrine as a consistent expression of the Christian idea that God is love. It has been easy for process theologians to build on these foundations. The two doctrines in question are those of the divine impassibility and of God's omnipotence.

The doctrine of impassibility is that God, being perfect, cannot be acted on by anything outside. Although certain biblical verses have been cited in its favor, in its systematic form it is clearly the product of the transformation of biblical thought in the Greek world. It arose in philosophical theology rather than from the study of the Bible. Yet it took deep hold on the mind of the church, so deep that it was little disturbed by the Reformation's effort to purify the biblical message of philosophical accretions.

Nevertheless, the idea has been vulnerable to criticism. It has existed alongside much Christian rhetoric that suggests the opposite. If taken with total seriousness, it would make nonsense of petitionary prayer. It did in fact encourage redirecting much such prayer to Jesus, then to Mary, and to Joseph and the saints. As the Reformers called for prayer to God the Father, the tension was intensified. Why pray to a God who can in no way be affected by our prayer?

The problem is not only with prayer. More broadly, why serve a God who is unaffected by our service? Why glorify a God who is unaffected by our glorification? Perhaps the widespread focus on rewards and punishments as the reason for obedience is one result of this teaching that nothing affects God. It provides another reason for praying, serving, and

glorifying, if these are understood to be divine command-
ments.

It is also hard to understand what " God loves us" means
if God is not affected by what happens to us. Since we human beings are affected deeply by what happens to those
we love, the divine love must be very different from all that
we come to know as love through human experience. Yet
the idea that God loves us is fundamental to the New Testament message. Thus the tension between the official doctrine
of divine impassibility and the real beliefs of most Christians,
informed by the Bible, is enormous.

The teaching itself was qualified from the beginning as it
was taken over from Greek philosophy. For Aristotle, divine
impassibility required God's ignorance of what transpires
in the world. For Christians this was not acceptable. God
must know what happens, and in that sense be affected by
events. The solution was to hold that God timelessly knows
all that has happened, now happens, and will happen, but
that this knowledge is not of the sort that involves passion,
that is, emotion.

Several theologians in the nineteenth century questioned
this doctrine, and the challenge to it has become a crescendo
in the twentieth century. Bonhoeffer is famous for his statement that only a suffering God can help. Quite independently,
the Japanese theologian Kitamori wrote of *The Pain of God*.
Jürgen Moltmann has developed this theme at great length.
Today it has become a commonplace of much theological
discourse.

Most of this could be understood in terms of purification
of biblical symbolism from Greek philosophical distortion.
But it is not only that. In each case, one can see contemporary influences at work on the theologians, influences that
function to transform the tradition as well as to purify it of
unwanted elements. The parallel work of process thinkers,
going back to the thirties, places the emphasis on the transformation. That is, it does not simply allow biblical symbol-

ism to express itself free from philosophical interference. It also uses these biblical insights in conjunction with fresh philosophical ones to develop a doctrine of God that shows both how God is vulnerable to what happens in the world and the respects in which the tradition correctly asserted that God is not affected. In other words, process theology does not treat the whole tradition from the second century to the twentieth as simply mistaken on this point.

Process theology develops a "di-polar" doctrine of God. There are respects, very important ones, in which God is changeless, and therefore "impassible" in the sense of being unaffected by the world. God is always, unalterably, knowing and loving, for example, and nothing that happens in the world can affect that fact. God's nature and character are immutable. The same is true of God's being, God's everlastingness, and God's all-inclusiveness. Hence one "pole" of God *is* impassible.

But if God is all-knowing and all-loving and all-inclusive, then the divine experience is continuously changing. That is, God is knowing and loving and including everything that occurs as it occurs. God did not love me until I came into being. God did not know just what would happen today until it happened. Thus the argument for God's impassibility applies only to one aspect of God. The traditional doctrine was one-sided, and because it treated that one side as if it were the whole reality, it was mistaken. But it had its truth, and that truth as well as the truth it obscured are both needed. This creative transformation of the tradition offers the church a needed way ahead.

In its critique of divine omnipotence as well, process theology has allies. Dietrich Bonhoeffer's statement that only a suffering God can help was opposed to the idea that it is an all-controlling God who helps. Many biblical scholars have shown that the power of God celebrated by Paul is a highly paradoxical one, contradicting the notions of power prevalent in the world. H. Richard Niebuhr developed this point beautifully in *The Meaning of Revelation*. Today, feminist theologians radically question the notion of controlling power that has been central to the idea of omnipotence. Nevertheless, on this topic many professional theologians as well as many laypeople cling to the idea that God is omnipotent.

Is omnipotence a biblical idea or one that emerged only in the synthesis of biblical and Greek thinking as was the case with divine impassibility? The answer here is more ambiguous. Nowhere in the Bible is divine omnipotence clearly asserted. The use of the term "almighty," so common in Genesis, Job, and Revelation, does not have this strict meaning. Yet there are many passages that attribute to God unilateral causation of particular events, and sometimes, by implication, of all events. On the other hand, there are many other passages in which human decisions are held to be responsible for what happens. The straightforward doctrine of divine omnipotence, namely, that God alone is responsible for everything that happens, just as it happens, gets some scattered support from particular biblical passages, but it is certainly not *the* biblical position. Much more prevalent are passages that indicate that there are real alternatives lying before human beings and that God acts differently according to how human beings choose among these options. This presents God as by far the most powerful actor, but certainly not the only one. What God does is often depicted as a response to what human beings do.

The most common interpretation of this situation today is to posit divine self-limitation. In this theory God is capable of determining everything but refrains from doing so in order to make space for human freedom. From the point of view of process theologians, this doctrine of the self-limitation of an omnipotent God does not succeed. It depicts a God who could control every detail but refrains from interfering even when humans engage in such horrible acts as the Holocaust. This is beyond understanding. Why not a little intervention now and then? Surely an all-powerful God could manage that without fundamentally undermining human freedom! And surely the biblical depiction of God does not count against such interference!

For process theologians, as for feminists, the fundamental issue is not the quantity of power to be attributed to God but the nature of the power that is divine. Is it the ability to control others? Many seem to think so, especially men. But in fact very little that is positive can be accomplished by this kind of power. The most common image of God's relation to human beings in the New Testament is the parental one.

It is true that parents do have some coercive power over their children. They can physically force them to stay in a particular room or even force food down their throats. But when parents are reduced to these coercive actions, they recognize themselves as failures as parents, and as virtually impotent. If this becomes the major pattern in relations between parents and children, the results are disastrous for both. This is not the relation implied when Jesus addresses God as "Abba."

Short of this kind of coercion is the use of rewards and punishments. Parents have the power to punish disobedient children and to reward obedient ones. Punishments and rewards can come close to strict coercion when they become extreme. But once again, this exercise of parental power expresses failure rather than success.

What parents want is that their children become mature and responsible people able to make their own decisions and act upon them. The more parents employ controlling power, or rule by externally imposed punishments and rewards, the less likely is this outcome. To treat the occasionally necessary evil of total control, or governing with rewards and punishments, as the model for divine power appears to process theologians to be sacrilegious. This is very different indeed from the power of love, the power that liberates and empowers the one toward whom it is directed. We believe Christians should learn the meaning of God's power first from the cross of Christ and from the bond of love that made of the disciples friends of Jesus rather than slaves.

Of course, this is a complex topic. I have broached it here to indicate another example of transformation. That God's power is the power that frees, directs, and strengthens, indeed, the power that transforms, has much biblical basis. How do Christians relate this to other passages in which divine power seems to bind and disempower human beings? Process theologians read the whole of the Bible Christocentrically. Instead of interpreting Christ in categories that were established before the coming of Jesus, interpret the whole in light of what Jesus revealed about divine power.

When we do so, many other things fall into place. The tension between God's power and human freedom disappears. We cease to celebrate a type of power of which far too much has been exercised in human history, and we celebrate instead the form of power of which there can never be enough. We stop looking for divine intervention to solve our problems and seek God's help and strength and guidance in solving them ourselves.

But process theology does not agree with Bonhoeffer that *only* a suffering God can help, not if that means that only God's suffering helps. We desperately need an empowering and guiding and liberating God. We can learn to identify God's creative and redemptive activity within us and within the world, and we can give ourselves to working with it and finding it working in ourselves. There is much, very much, in our tradition that supports all this. The tradition needs to be purified of those other themes that inhibit the full and consistent affirmation of these. And this purified tradition can be integrated with the insights of feminists and others in a creative transformation that is already taking place. (See Anna Case-Winters, *God's Power*. Westminster/John Knox Press.)

For the process of transformation there are no fixed rules that all Christians are prepared to accept. The way of transforming may sometimes need to be transformed. But for me, now, Christ is central. For others, perhaps, the authority of the Bible, or the classical creeds, or the liberation of women, or the renewal of the congregation is central. Only as we talk honestly about what it means to us to think intentionally *as Christians* about important matters can an open and fruitful dialogue begin.

The Problem of Evil

The problem that most often leads lay Christians to raise theological questions is the vivid experience of evil. When one is personally struck with suffering one asks: why? Why does this happen to me? Unless the creative transformation of the doctrine of God is relevant to us in that situation, it remains, for many Christians, too abstract to evoke serious concern. Since the purpose of this chapter is to bring lay theology and church theology close together, it will conclude with reflection on this topic.

The question "Why?" does not arise only among Christians. The sense that what happens in life should be just is very widespread. Buddhists sometimes answer the question in terms of *karma*. If what happens in this life seems entirely unjust, some Buddhists will explain that it is in response to evil done in previous lives.

The question is intensified by traditional Christian teaching. If God is omnipotent in the strictest sense, that is, if God is the immediate cause of all that happens, then the evil that befalls one is directly inflicted by God. If God is righteous, then there must be a morally adequate reason for this suffering.

The simplest explanation is that one has deserved it. Only if one is guilty of terrible crimes can the suffering be justified. Thus, added to the immediate suffering is the recognition of one's guilt, even when one is not sure of what one is guilty.

To avoid the compounding of suffering with guilt, some argue that God has a purpose in inflicting this suffering other than punishment. It may bring others to repentance or be an occasion of spiritual growth for all. Even if no adequate gain can be discerned, this does not prove that the omniscient one has no overarching plan within which what humans see as unnecessary and unjust evil in fact works for the greater good.

The recent modification of divine omnipotence through the doctrine of divine self-limitation has quite different consequences for the understanding of evil. In this view God does not inflict the suffering. It arises through natural and human causes. God allows these causes to work themselves out. God could interfere, but greater good is attained when God does not do so. The person who suffers may, or may not, share in the responsibility for the suffering. The suffering may, or may not, have the potentiality of effecting some good. In any case, human beings should do all that they can to alleviate suffering and to try to bring about a situation in which less suffering occurs.

Process theologians do not accept the view that God has at every moment the capacity to set things right but never does so. The sufferer can receive little comfort from the view that God could save but does not do so. But we accept much of the rest of what is said. The causes of suffering include natural and human factors. One should not ask why God has inflicted this suffering since that presupposes unilateral determination by God.

Nevertheless, the view of process theologians with regard to how God relates to evil is quite different from those who speak of the self-limitation of an omnipotent God. God does not stand by idly observing the suffering. God is present and active in every event seeking to bring out of it what good can be obtained. God is present and active in the healing powers of the body and the mind and in the love of friends and the skill of physicians. God is empowering the sufferer

to endure the suffering and to find some silver lining, however thin. God is also present as "the fellow sufferer who
understands." (Alfred North Whitehead, *Process and Reality*,
corrected edition by David Griffin and Donald Sherburne.
New York: The Free Press, 1978, p. 351.) In short, what God
can do, God is doing, and although that often does not include removal of the evil, it is still a great deal. And as we
recognize what God is doing, attend to it in gratitude, and
open ourselves to it, what God can do becomes greater. Sometimes this even results in the overcoming of the evil.

Sometimes the evil that raises theological questions is not
so intimately personal. Sometimes it is the evil of war in some
other part of the world, of the oppression and exploitation
of the poor, of the degradation of the planet. How can a good
and powerful God cause or allow such global horrors?

Even for process theologians, this question is not easily
answered. It becomes, for us, the question: if God is working
everywhere for the good, why does evil seem so largely to
prevail?

The answer for us is that evil is ultimately parasitic of
good. Through the evolutionary process God has brought
into being sentient beings. This is a great good. Without them
the world would be a poor place indeed. But sentient beings
are capable of pain as well as pleasure, of suffering as well as
joy. Furthering the maintenance of the life of some requires
the suffering death of others.

Even more important, God has brought into being human beings. That, too, is a great good. A planet without us
would be greatly impoverished. But our greatness also involves our unique capacities for destruction.

God calls us, urges us, to use our power for good. Much
of the time, many of us do in fact act in generosity and love.
It is not true that we are on the whole simply wicked and
destructive. But our power of destruction is so great that
when through ignorance, disease, or sin, we do undertake to
destroy one another or our habitat, our rejection of God's

call is horrendously effective. What is built up over centuries, millennia, or millions of years can be destroyed in a day or a year. God is not destroyed. Much that is good in the creation remains, but the suffering is enormous and the setback to God's purposes can be vast.

Our hope lies in God. Apart from God's universal creative-redemptive work we are doomed. But that work takes place through creatures who are only partly responsive. There is no assurance that we will allow it to triumph through us. How we respond to God's call determines what kind of world we will pass on to our descendants—or even whether there will be any human descendants at all.

Conclusion

This chapter is not a call for lay theology alone. The transformation of the tradition requires a knowledge of the tradition that is more accessible to those who specialize in the study of that tradition than to Christian laypeople in general. In this way it differs from the two preceding chapters.

But even if laypeople depend in part on professionals for the transformation of the tradition, they need not stand aside and leave this task to others. The problems with the tradition are not esoteric ones apparent only to specialists. Laypeople are aware, or easily become aware, of many of these problems. If they do not wrestle with them and come to new views, changes in official church teaching or among a professional elite will do little good. Only a partnership between professional and lay theologians will serve to heal and enliven the thinking of the church.

This chapter has invited laypeople into a discussion that is too often carried on in separation from the ordinary life of the church. It is a discussion in which they can and should take part. The issues impinge on the life of the church and of individual Christians. Practical Christian thinking flows naturally into these questions. It can inform them and be informed by new answers. In that interaction lies the hope for the creative transformation of the church.

Afterword

On Academic Theology

This book has been written against the hegemony of academic theology. Few things are more important for the church today than to reclaim theology for laypeople and to engage them in the tasks they can do best. But it would be unfortunate if my book left the impression that academic theology were not also, often, intentional Christian thinking about important matters.

The intellectual tradition in which most academic theology of the oldline denominations stands is an extremely important one. It is the tradition that has taken seriously the profound intellectual changes that have taken place in the modern world and has undertaken to rethink the Christian faith in view of these changes. Had there been no such tradition, thoughtful and sensitive people would now find it almost impossible to take Christian beliefs seriously.

The problem is that many of the challenges to Christian faith have been raised through philosophical reflection that is still remote to those who have not been extensively exposed to it. This includes most laypeople. Thus the theological response is equally remote. Indirectly, laypeople are profoundly affected by the intellectual changes brought about through Hume, Kant, Hegel, Feuerbach, Marx, and Nietzsche, and in this sense the theological responses to their thought are highly relevant. But these effects are difficult to bring to consciousness, and the complex history is hard to summarize usefully for those who do not have the time and inclination to engage themselves with it. Also the diversity of views on the part of academic theologians who are heirs of this theological tradition is so great, and the disagreements among them so fundamental, that it is hard to see much gain from trying to draw a large number of Christian laity into these debates in their present form.

The situation is made more difficult today by the fact that many professionals in theological schools understand their calling in disciplinary terms and not as theology in the sense defined in this book. They are thinking about matters of great importance, but the perspective from which they think is not intentionally Christian. They bring to bear fruitful methods that expose evils in the Christian tradition of which we need to repent, but the scholars do not always assume responsibility for helping the church engage in appropriate repentance.

Fortunately, some developments of academic theology do make contact with church theology from time to time, even in its lay form. Most important are those academic theologians who have associated themselves with one or another of the liberation theologies. The discussion in Chapter 4 of creative transformation and renewal as two models for what the church should be doing today are also influenced by developments in academic theology, but are accessible to laypeople.

In addition there are other possibilities. The question of how Christians should view other religious communities has come up several times in this book. This is a question that arises quite naturally in lay theology. It is one that has played a significant role in academic theology for two centuries. Academic theologians familiar with this history can work with lay theologians to clarify some of the options, but not to pronounce solutions for laypeople to accept on authority.

There is also some rethinking of academic theology in light of what is called the new physics. This makes contact with a good deal of popular writing in our society. There is real potential for uniting academic and lay theology around some of the new possibilities brought forward in this way, especially when both take the environmental crisis seriously. Although this is today at the fringe of both academic theology and church theology, there are signs of increased interest. It *could* become a new intersection of academic and church theology, one in which laypeople could give a great deal of leadership without excluding the contributions of professionals.

Academic theology should not be dismissed in an effort to renew lay theology. The church would be impoverished indeed without professionals who are able to remain abreast of the intellecutal currents of our time and to represent Christian scholarship and faith in that context. The church would be much better off if more of its pastors could take part in that work. This activity is *not* irrelevant even when it remains separate from church theology.

But the goal is to reintegrate the several types of theology, so that lay theology can do its crucial work in ways that are appropriate to the present state of the intellectual and cultural discussion. This has happened in the past. It can happen in the future. It is not likely to happen unless laypeople reclaim the theological task soon in whatever ways are accessible and meaningful to them. It is also not likely to happen unless church professionals want it to happen and order their priorities so as to facilitate its happening.

For Further Reading

John B. Cobb, Jr., *Becoming a Thinking Christian* (Nashville: Abingdon Press, 1993). A guidebook for laypeople on how to go about doing what the present book discusses.

John B. Cobb, Jr., *Can Christ Become Good News Again?* (St. Louis: Chalice Press, 1991). A collection of essays and addresses dealing with a multiplicity of subjects in the area of practical Christian thinking.

John B. Cobb, Jr., *Matters of Life and Death* (Louisville: Westminster/John Knox Press, 1991). A succinct exploration of four crucial issues of our time: environmental destruction, suicide, abortion, and human sexuality.

John B. Cobb, Jr., *Praying for Jennifer* (Nashville: The Upper Room, 1985). A discussion of different theologies of prayer in story form.

Robert Mesle, *Process Theology: A Basic Introduction* (St. Louis: Chalice Press, 1993). A very readable introduction to the theological point of view expressed in Chapter Four of this book.

David P. Polk, ed., *What's a Christian to Do?* (St. Louis: Chalice Press, 1991). Explores six tough issues facing Christians today in an innovative format that invites theological reflection.

David P. Polk, ed., *Now What's a Christian to Do?* (St. Louis: Chalice Press, 1994). A sequel to the preceding volume, with six additional topics developed in the same useful format.